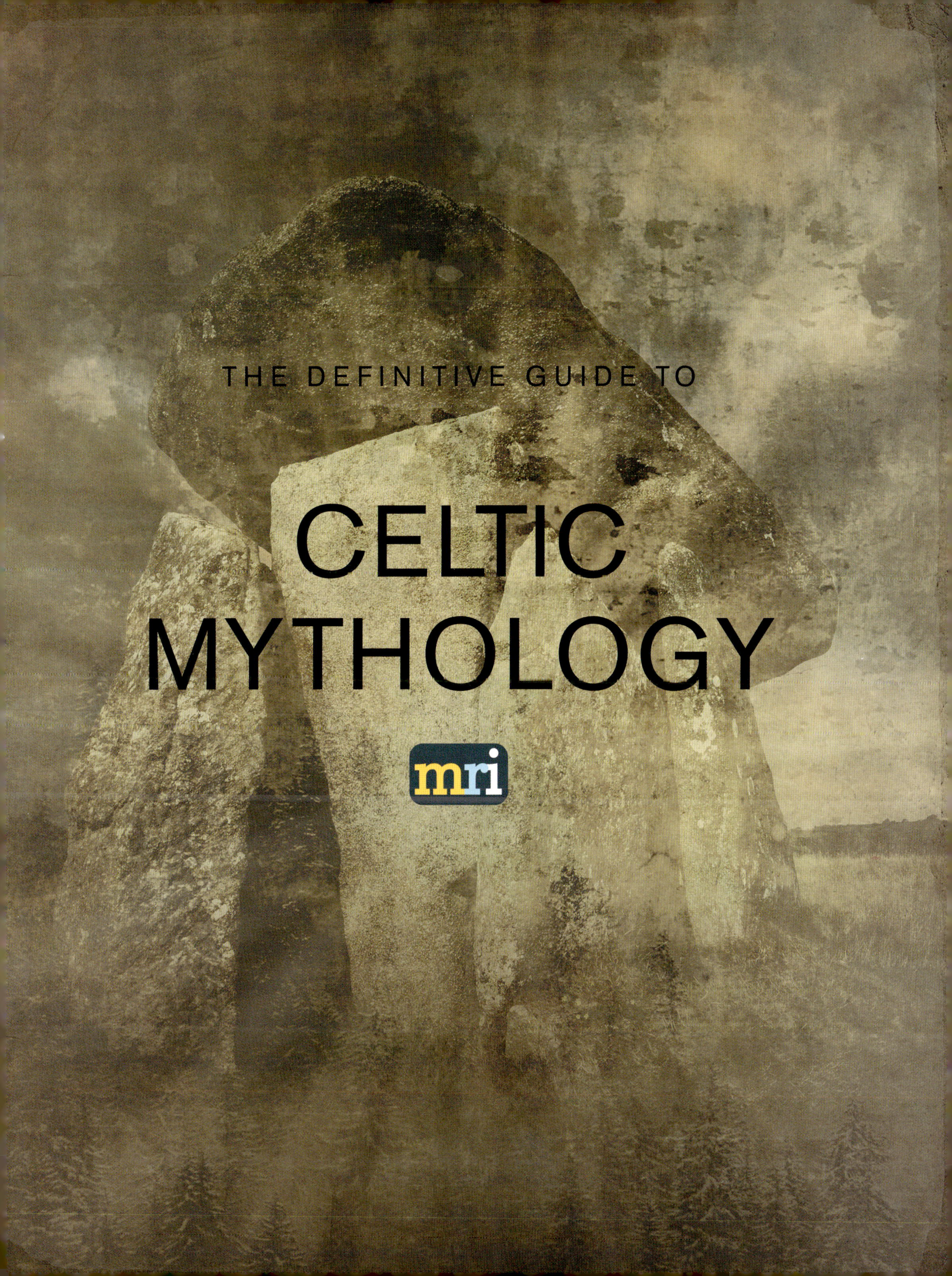

THE DEFINITIVE GUIDE TO

CELTIC MYTHOLOGY

MOSELEY ROAD INTERNATIONAL
International Rights and Packaging
www.moseleyroad.com.

President Sean Moore

International Rights Karen Prince
kprince@moseleyroad.com

Written by Finn D. Moore | Edited by Duncan Youel

Series Management: Oiloften.co.uk
Picture research and book design: Duncan Youel

Other titles in the series:
The Mythology of Ancient Egypt | The Mythology of Ancient Greece | Norse Mythology

Printed and bound in China

ISBN 978-1-62669-232-9

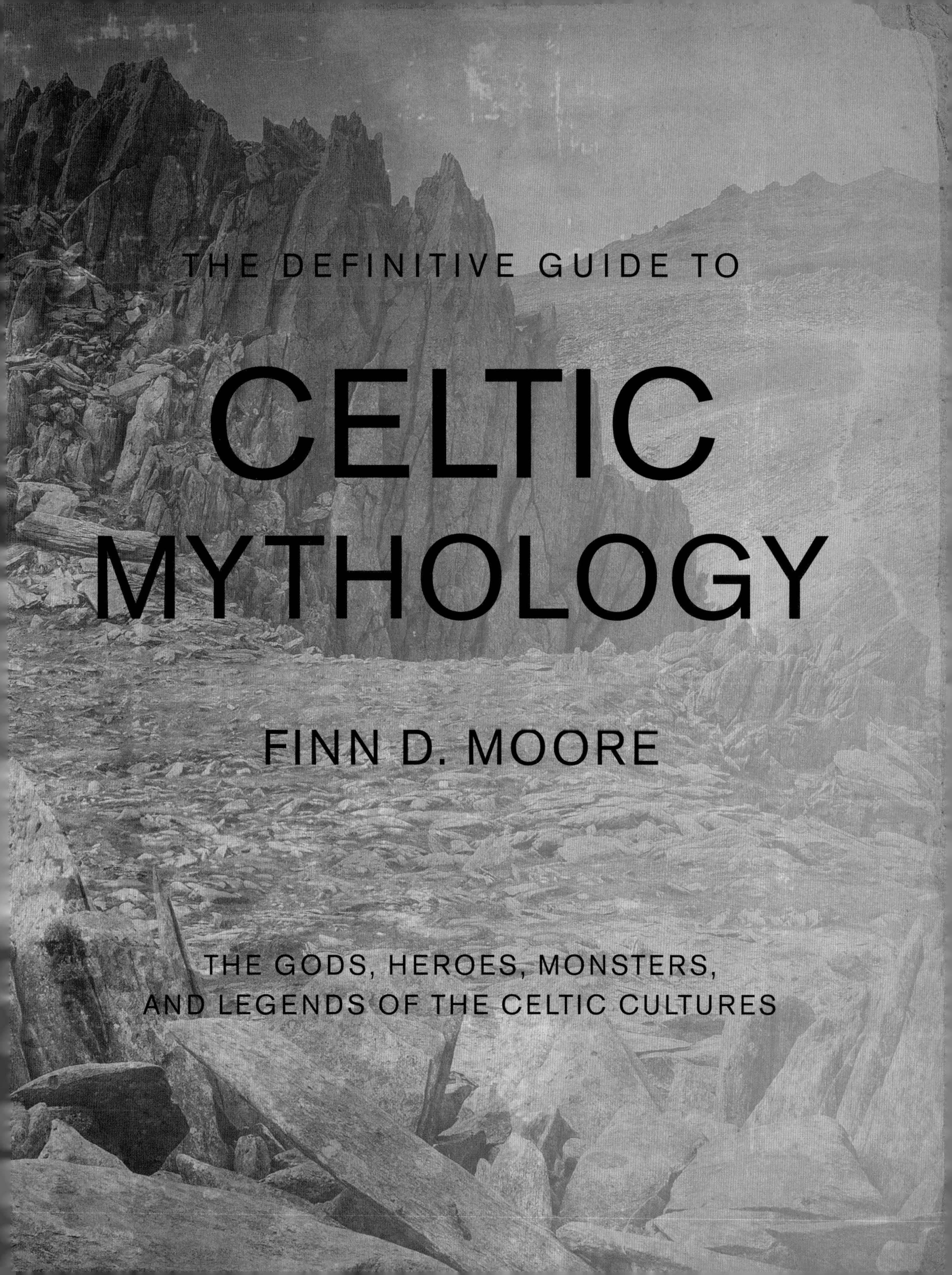

THE DEFINITIVE GUIDE TO

CELTIC MYTHOLOGY

FINN D. MOORE

THE GODS, HEROES, MONSTERS, AND LEGENDS OF THE CELTIC CULTURES

CONTENTS

The ancient and mysterious Celtic civilization evolved and developed during the Iron Age migration of peoples from Central Europe, first to the Iberian Peninsula, then to their arrival on the temperate Atlantic shores of France and the British Isles.

CELTIC CULTURE

Above: This 1620 map, tracing the territories of Europe at the height of the Roman Empire, also allows us to picture the movement of the Celtic peoples: From Central Europe, tribes went southeast into Anatolia (modern Turkey), but mainly west into northern Italy; then southwest into the Iberian Peninsula (Spain and Portugal); northwest into France; and finally, into the British Isles. It's also thought that migrations back across the English Channel occurred—into Breton, (Brittany), as Angles and Saxons began to move into England; **Opposite:** A 17th century map of *Ancient Hiberniae*: Ireland. For fifteen hundred years and more, until Saint Patrick and the advent of Christianity in the 5th century AD, it's one of the principal cultural centers of the Celtic tribes.

HIBERNIÆ
REGNUM
tam in præcipuas
ULTONIÆ, CONNACIÆ,
LACENIÆ, et MOMONIÆ,
quam in minores earundem Provincias
et Ditiones divisum
IOH. BAPT. HOMANNO
Norimbergæ
THE IRISH SEA OR ST. GEORGES CHANNEL
ULSTER
MUNSTER

NOTES ON CELTIC REVIVALS

Celtic mythology has been revived and reinterpreted several times over the centuries, driven by events that have caused many to rediscover and reimagine their Celtic heritage.

Above: William Butler Yeats by Alice Broughton, Published in the *Gaelic American* on 5 March 1904; **Top:** Lady Charlotte Guest. Her translation of the *Mabinogion* was the first to be published in modern print format. It was published in English and Welsh in seven volumes between 1838 and 1845.

The Celtic revival of the 18th and 19th centuries, like the equivalent renewal of interest in the Old Nordic universe in Germany and Scandinavia, and the cultural themes of the Romantic Age, all coincided with the burgeoning mechanical industrialization of Western Europe. Each could be said to be a distinctly human response to this quickening of the pace of change, and of encroaching science, technology and capital that would transform human existence. Something we still struggle with. Today those ancient Celtic stories still exert a significant pull on the threads of popular culture, calling us back.

The corpus of these early myths has even become the intellectual and emotional landscape for neo-pagans, reflecting a deep need to be in tune with the rhythms of the Earth, and to find a way of living that is not driven by the incessant needs of a consumerist society which holds us all in its thrall.

The Celtic Revival, also known as the Celtic Renaissance, first emerged in the late 18th century as an artistic and literary movement that at once romanticized Celtic identity, particularly in Ireland, Wales, and Scotland. In the British Isles, this revival was fueled by a growing interest in preserving and reclaiming national heritage, particularly in the face of the dominant *English* cultural and political orthodoxy.

Writers, poets, and artists from these old Celtic nations found a spiritual nourishment and inspiration in their deep mythological past, bringing the tales of Cú Chulainn, Fionn mac Cumhaill, and the *Mabinogion* to a broader audience. Key figures like James Macpherson, Lady Charlotte Guest, William Butler Yeats, and Lady Gregory, were instrumental in popularizing these narratives. This movement helped re-establish Celtic mythology as a celebrated part of cultural identity, especially in Ireland, where it soon became associated with the nation's struggle for independence and cultural revitalization.

Meanwhile, in England, Arthurian legend (with its original incarnation rooted in Welsh mythology), also experienced a significant revival. Authors and poets like Alfred, Lord Tennyson, and later T.H. White, contributed to the reimagining of King Arthur's court, and the chivalric ideals which had been associated with it. In Victorian England, artists and designers such as Edward Burne-Jones, William Morris, John William Waterhouse, and William Dyce all returned to the subject time and again. For Burne-Jones, King Arthur became something of an obsession. For William Morris, the "Golden Age

of Chivalry," in the idyllic pre-Modern pastorale of Arthurian legend, entwined with his socialist aesthetic to produce the Arts and Crafts Movement. By the end of the 19th century, Maesteg-born painter Christopher Williams was regularly finding his inspiration in the *Mabinogion*.

In recent decades, neo-paganism and modern Druidic practices have drawn heavily from Celtic mythology, seeking spiritual inspiration and succor from the beliefs and practices of the ancient Celts. Neo-pagan groups often integrate myths and symbols from Irish, Welsh, and broader Celtic sources, incorporating deities like Brigid, Lugh, and the Morrigan into their pantheon and celebrating festivals such as Samhain, Imbolc, and Beltane.

Many neo-pagan traditions interpret Celtic mythology as part of a reconstructed belief system focused on nature, seasonal cycles, and a connection with the Otherworld.

In today's 24 hour online world, Celtic mythology pops up everywhere: in modern literature; platform adventure game franchises; film and television; art; design... and also in the real world...as fashionable body art. Celtic symbolism vies with Old Norse and Viking runes for popularity in today's tattoo studios.

Elements of Irish and Scottish landscapes are frequently the settings referenced in film and video game culture, specifically to evoke approximations of mystical and otherworldly qualities, and Irish fairy folklore has been popularized through the young adult fantasy novels of Holly Black's *The Folk of the Air* series, weaving into its pages, as it does, *changelings* and *kelpies* alongside the *Aos Sí*. The animated movie *The Secret of the Kells* and platform franchise *King Arthur* mix Magic into the pixels—coding the visual and surface signs of the old world mythology into the means of modern entertainment.

Above: Edward Burne-Jones (left) and William Morris, photographed by Frederick H. Hollyer, 1874; **Top:** *Ancient British Celts*, an 1836 interpretation of a Celtic family. A steel engraving by sculptor J. Rogers.

SOURCES AND CHALLENGES

Existing sources of Celtic mythology are a blend of oral tradition, medieval manuscript preservation, and later scholarly interpretations.

The Celts primarily passed down their stories orally, and only a fraction of these tales subsequently survive in written form. The reliance on oral transmission means that many myths were altered over time, reshaped by each storyteller and region.

A particular challenge in studying Celtic mythology is to disentangle the 'overwriting' of successive, external cultures, including Roman, Anglo-Saxon, Norse, and Norman. Each of these peoples left its mark on the local traditions, influencing how the myths were remembered and recorded.

The influence of Christian scribes was perhaps the most transformative, as they often reinterpreted gods as saints, otherworldly beings as demonic, and heroes as virtuous figures. As a result, understanding the original intent and meaning behind these myths requires careful analysis of the context in which they were written.

The primary sources of Celtic mythology that survive today are medieval manuscripts, written centuries after the myths originated. For Irish mythology, some of the most valuable texts include the *Lebor Gabála Érenn* (*Book of Invasions*), *Cath Maige Tuired* (*The Second Battle of Moytura*), and the *Dindshenchas*, which recounts the lore of Ireland's sacred sites. *The Book of Leinster* and the *Book of Ballymote* also provide insight into the mythological and heroic tales of Ireland, particularly those related to the Mythological, Ulster, Fenian, and Historical Cycles.

However, these manuscripts were written primarily by Christian monks who sought to preserve Ireland's oral tradition but often reinterpreted or modified the myths to align with Christian values, leading to the blending of pagan and Christian elements.

In Welsh mythology, the primary collection of sources is the *Mabinogion*, a series of prose tales that were recorded in the *White Book of Rhydderch* and the *Red Book of Hergest*. These tales capture elements of Welsh folklore and legend, including the Four Branches, which depict complex interactions between human and otherworldly figures, as well as early stories associated with the Arthurian tradition. Like the Irish manuscripts, these Welsh texts were also transcribed by Christian monks, which resulted in the reinterpretation of certain characters and themes. This Christianized context sometimes masks the original nature of the myths, especially with figures like Pwyll, Rhiannon, and Bran, who likely had greater significance in pre-Christian Welsh beliefs. For Cornish and Breton mythology, written sources are even scarcer. Legends were primarily passed down through folk traditions and oral storytelling, and few were formally recorded before the modern period.

Opposite left: The Roman fleet landing at the River Medway in Kent, during Claudius's invasion of Britain in 43 AD. Painting for postcard series by the military artist Harry Payne, London, 1900s; **Opposite right:** Boadicea (or Boudicca) the Celtic Iceni tribe queen who fought the Roman invaders around London and St. Albans; **Above left:** Angles and Saxons from the north European mainland began incursions into East Anglia after the Roman evacuation in 409 AD; **Above right:** Children's book illustration of the Battle of Hastings, fought on 14 October 1066 between the English army of the Anglo-Saxon King, Harold Godwinson, and the Norman army of William, Duke of Normandy. The decisive victory by the French began the Norman Conquest of England; **Top right:** Christian monks transcribed the ancient spoken stories, embellishing and shaping their context.

THE HISTORICAL CONTEXT

Celtic mythology is deeply intertwined with the cultural, historical, and geographical landscapes of the ancient Celtic peoples. These myths, woven from a mixture of oral tradition and written preservation, reflect the lives, beliefs, and struggles of a complex and far-reaching civilization.

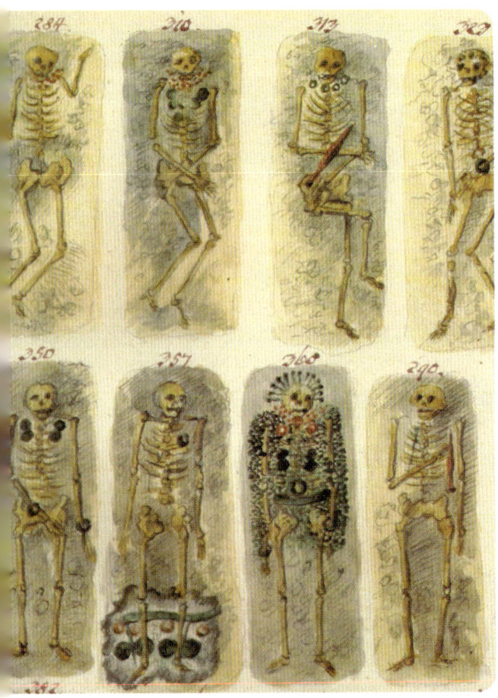

Above: Sketch notations made by Johann Georg Ramsauer, during the excavation of the ancient cemetery he discovered near Halstatt in 1846. The town gave its name to the earliest-known tribe of the Celtic civilization

The Celts were not a unified political entity but a network of tribes spread across the European continent. From their origins in central Europe to their expansion across the British Isles, the Celts developed a rich cultural identity that combined elements of their environment, interactions with other societies, and unique spiritual worldviews. To fully appreciate Celtic mythology, one must first understand the historical context in which it was born and evolved.

THE ORIGINS AND SPREAD OF THE CELTS

The term "Celtic" refers to a collection of related languages, cultures, and peoples rather than a single nation or ethnicity. The earliest evidence of Celtic culture is found in the Hallstatt culture (circa 1200–500 BC), named after an archaeological site in Austria. This early Iron Age culture was marked by advanced metalwork, particularly in bronze and iron, and elaborate burial practices. Hallstatt burials often included rich funerary goods, suggesting a stratified society with a warrior aristocracy.

By the 6th century BC, the Celts entered their second major cultural phase, known as the La Tène culture (circa 500–50 BC). Originating near Lake Neuchâtel in Switzerland, the La Tène culture is characterized by its intricate art style, featuring flowing curves, spirals, and motifs inspired by nature. This period marked the height of Celtic expansion, as tribes migrated westward into Iberia, Gaul (modern-day France), and the British Isles, while others moved southeast into northern Italy and even as far as Anatolia (modern Turkey), where they became known as the Galatians.

The British Isles became one of the most significant centers of Celtic culture and mythology. By the late Iron Age, the Celts had established a stronghold in Ireland,

Britain, and Scotland, where their myths and practices flourished. The relative geographical separation of the British Isles allowed many of these traditions to survive longer than on the European mainland, as Roman and Christian influences there began to infiltrate and transform Celtic society.

The Celts' migrations brought them into contact with numerous cultures, including the Greeks, Etruscans, and later the Romans. Greek writers, such as Herodotus, described the Celts as a distinct and widespread people, and archaeological evidence supports their extensive trade networks. These interactions influenced Celtic material culture and likely their mythology, blending indigenous beliefs with ideas borrowed from their neighbors.

Above: The Celtic head sculpture discovered in the prehistoric earthworks at Mšecké Žehrovice, some 65 km northwest of Prague, Czech Republic. The cretaceous limestone head from the La Tene culture dates from circa 300 BC. Courtesy of the Narodni muzeum in Prague, Czech Republic; **Above left:** The earthworks at Mšecké Žehrovice; **Top left:** Oppidum Zavist, the Celtic Hillfort south of Prague, a polycultural archaeological site by the Vltava river, most notably of the Halstatt and La Tene cultures; **Top right:** Ladder uncovered during the excavation of the Celtic salt mines in Hallstatt, Salzkammergut, Austria

Above: Cernunnos on the Pillar of the Boatmen, courtesy of the Museum of the Middle Ages, Paris France; **Top:** Remains of the Santa Tegra "castro" (an "oppidum," or hillfort community) in Galicia, Spain (Castro na ladeira do Monte de Santa Tegra, Provincia de Pontevedra, Galicia.) Circa 300–100 BC, Courtesy of Henrique Pereira

CELTIC EUROPE

As the Celts moved into new territories, they carried their cultural and spiritual practices with them, adapting them to local contexts. In Gaul, the Celts established a vibrant culture that maintained many of the hallmarks of their mythology and religious beliefs. The Gaulish Celts worshiped a pantheon of deities, some of whom paralleled Irish and British gods, while others were unique to the region. For example, Cernunnos, a horned god associated with animals and fertility, appears frequently in Gaulish art and inscriptions.

The Gaulish Celts also integrated their myths into their political and military practices. Chieftains and warriors were often seen as representatives of divine power, and myths about gods and heroes were used to legitimize their authority. This intertwining of mythology and rulership helped reinforce social hierarchies and fostered unity among the tribes.

In the Iberian Peninsula, particularly in northern regions like Galicia and Asturias, Celtic influence is evident in both archaeological finds and folklore. The Celtiberians, who inhabited parts of modern Spain and Portugal, had their own deities and mythological traditions, many of which mirrored broader Celtic themes of nature, fertility, and heroism. Artifacts such as stone carvings and votive offerings reflect a shared spiritual focus on the cycles of life and death.

The Celts also inherited many prehistoric monuments from earlier cultures. Sites like Stonehenge and Avebury in England, though built long before the Celts, can be viewed as ancestors of the standing stones and megalithic monuments that later became a core symbol of Celtic culture.

THE CELTS IN EASTERN EUROPE AND ANATOLIA

The southeastward expansion of the Celts brought their culture into contact with regions as far as Anatolia. By the 3rd century BC, a group of Celts known as the Galatians had migrated through the Balkans into modern Turkey. There, they established settlements and interacted with Hellenistic cultures, blending Celtic and Greek traditions. While much of their original mythology was likely altered or lost due to this cultural exchange, traces of Celtic influence appear in their art, burial practices, and accounts from Greek historians.

In Eastern Europe, Celtic tribes left a legacy of burial sites and artifacts, including weapons, jewelry, and religious objects. The Celts' presence in these regions helped spread their artistic and religious motifs, many of which would influence neighboring cultures. For instance, the Celts' use of animal symbolism and their reverence for nature resonated with other Indo-European traditions, creating shared themes in regional folklore.

Top: Reedbeds, Lake Neuchâtel, Switzerland. Celtic votive offerings were frequently made in lakes; **Above left, top to bottom:** Votive offerings, all circa 300 BC: Ram (Sempt, Upper Bavaria); Boar (Lindau/Bodensee, Swabia); and Bull (Manching, Upper Bavaria), from the State Archaeological Collection, Munich; **Above right:** Celtic bronze bracelets, circa 300 BC. Narodni muzeum, Prague, Czech Republic.

Top left: *Vercingétorix throws down his arms at the feet of Julius Caesar*, by Lionel Royer, 1899. The surrender of the Gallic chieftain after the Battle of Alesia, in 52 BC. Today, many of the visual details in Royer's work are disputed; **Above left:** The cover of a 1946 edition of Julius Caesar's personal account of the Gallic Wars, *Commentarii de Bello Gallico*; **Above right:** The huge, heroic scale statue of Vercingétorix, by the French sculptor Aimé Millet. The monument is dedicated to the Gaulish chieftain Vercingétorix, who was defeated by Julius Caesar in the decisive Battle of Alesia in 52 BC. Commissioned by Napoleon III, it was completed in 1865, and stands on Mont Auxois, by Alise-Sainte-Reine in Burgundy, eastern France, on the site of the *oppidum* (hillfort) of Alesia.

The expansion of the Roman Empire into Celtic territories during the 1st century BC marked a turning point in the history of the Celts...

ROMAN CONQUEST AND CULTURAL TRANSFORMATION

Julius Caesar's conquest of Gaul, detailed in his *Commentarii de Bello Gallico*, provides one of the most comprehensive accounts of Celtic society, though heavily biased and aimed at justifying Roman imperialism. Under Roman rule, many aspects of Celtic culture were suppressed or assimilated. Roman governance, urbanization, and religious practices began to reshape the cultural landscape, particularly in Gaul and Britain.

Despite this, elements of Celtic religion persisted. Many Celtic deities were syncretized with Roman gods, blending local traditions with Roman practices. For example, the Irish god Lugh, associated with skill and craftsmanship, was often compared to Mercury, while Brigid, a goddess of healing and fertility, was linked to Minerva. Celtic sacred sites, such as springs and groves, were often repurposed as Roman temples, preserving their spiritual significance even under new religious frameworks.

In Ireland, which was never fully conquered by Rome, Celtic traditions endured more robustly. However, the advent of Christianity in the 4th and 5th centuries brought further changes to Celtic mythology. Christian missionaries, including Saint Patrick, converted much of the population, leading to a reinterpretation of Celtic myths through a Christian lens. Many gods and heroes were reimagined as saints or demons, and sacred festivals like Samhain were incorporated into Christian traditions, becoming All Hallows' Eve, or Halloween.

Above: A 19th century map of the Roman Empire in circa 33–100 AD. The Romans ruled "Britannia" until the evacuation of the legions in 409 AD, when they needed to defend their European mainland territories from the invading Franks. In 486 AD, the Franks defeated the last Roman authority in Gaul at the Battle of Soissons and Gaul came under the rule of the Merovingians, the first kings of a proto-France.

CELTIC COSMOLOGY AND OTHERWORLDS

Celtic cosmology is a fascinating and complex system that reflects the ancient Celts' understanding of the universe, life, and the divine.

Above: A summer thunderstorm in the agricultural heart of Wales, courtesy BBC Weather; **Top:** *Llyn Tegid* (Bala Lake), Gwynedd. An iconic Celtic location, see pages 152–153. Photograph by Simon Stapley at Alamy

At its heart lies the belief in a world that is layered and interconnected, with boundaries between the physical world, the spirit realm, and the Otherworld existing as fluid and permeable. This cosmology, rich in symbolism and reverence for nature, permeates Celtic mythology, in which realms, gods, and spirits interact closely with human existence.

Central to Celtic cosmology is the concept of three realms—earth, sea, and sky. These realms represented not only physical environments but also spiritual elements that structured existence. The Celts revered natural elements and saw each realm as infused with life, spirit, and energy. Deities were often associated with these realms, such as Manannán mac Lir, who ruled over the seas, and Lugh, connected with the skies and storms. This tripartite worldview extended to their understanding of time and existence, which the Celts viewed as cyclical rather than linear. Life, death, and rebirth were interconnected, with the physical and spiritual worlds constantly influencing one another.

One of the most intriguing aspects of Celtic cosmology is the Otherworld, a mystical realm that exists parallel to the human world. Known by various names, such as Tír na nÓg in Irish mythology, Annwn in Welsh mythology, and Avalon in Arthurian legend, the Otherworld was seen as a place of beauty, abundance,

and eternal youth. The Otherworld was neither heaven nor hell, as in Christian cosmology, but a land of mystery and magic where the souls of the dead, deities, and supernatural beings resided. While the Otherworld's inhabitants were largely benevolent, they could be capricious or even fearsome, requiring respect from those who encountered them. It was also accessible to the living, especially during liminal times and sacred festivals, such as Samhain, when the boundary between worlds was believed to weaken.

Access to the Otherworld often came through natural features such as mounds, caves, and bodies of water. These *sídhe* mounds, or fairy hills, were viewed as portals through which spirits and gods could enter the human realm. Rivers and lakes, particularly in Irish mythology, served as liminal spaces where mortals could encounter supernatural beings or cross into the Otherworld. Heroes and warriors, like Cú Chulainn and Oisín, ventured to the Otherworld on quests, emerging either transformed or tragically aware of the temporal nature of human life. The Otherworld was seen as both beautiful and dangerous, a place where wisdom and blessings could be gained, but from which few returned unchanged.

Main image, top: Aerial view of the great Knowth tumulus, part of the major Brú na Bóinne (Valley of the Boyne) complex in County Meath, Ireland, around 40km north of Dublin. The site is one of the world's most important prehistoric landscapes and includes the three large sacred passage graves of Knowth, Newgrange and Dowth, as well as some ninety additional monuments. Since 1993, a World Heritage Site, designated by UNESCO. See also pages 32–33; **Right:** Oisín and Niamh arrive in Tír na nÓg—the Land of Eternal Youth—on Niamh's magical steed. Illustration by Stephen Reid from *Myths & Legends of the Celtic Race* by Thomas Rolleston, 1911

ART, ARCHAEOLOGY, AND ARTIFACTS

As with all early civilizations, Celtic art is rich in symbolic motifs that convey mythological and religious themes

Top left: Danebury Hillfort in Hampshire, England; **Top right**: Close-up of the Battersea Shield; **Above:** The signature Celtic triskele spiral design

The triskele, for example, is often interpreted as representing the tripartite nature of the world (earth, sea, and sky) or the three stages of life (birth, life, and death). The knotwork patterns, with their endless loops, symbolize eternity and the cyclical nature of existence. Animal motifs, such as the stag, boar, and bird, are frequently depicted and are associated with various deities and mythological narratives.

ARCHAEOLOGICAL DISCOVERIES

Archaeological excavations across Europe have unearthed numerous sites and artifacts that shed light on Celtic mythology and religious practices. These discoveries provide tangible evidence of the Celts' reverence for their gods and the rituals they performed to honor them.

HILLFORTS AND SACRED SITES

Hillforts, such as Danebury in England and the oppidum of Bibracte in France, were central to Celtic society. These fortified settlements served not only as defensive structures but also as centers of trade, governance, and religious activity. Excavations at these sites have revealed altars, votive offerings, and other ritual objects, indicating the importance of religious practices in everyday life.

Sacred sites, such as the sanctuary of Roquepertuse in southern France, provide further evidence of Celtic religious activity. Roquepertuse is notable for its carved stone heads and statues, which are believed to represent deities or ancestral spirits. The site also features a large stone altar, suggesting that it was a place of communal worship and sacrifice.

BURIAL PRACTICES

Celtic burial practices offer valuable insights into their beliefs about the afterlife and the role of mythological figures in guiding the dead. The Hallstatt and La Tène cultures are known for their elaborate burial mounds, or tumuli, which often contain rich grave goods, including weapons, jewelry, and chariots. The Hochdorf Chieftain's Grave in Germany is a prime example of a high-status Celtic burial. Discovered in 1978, the grave dates to around 530 BC and contains a wealth of artifacts, including a bronze couch, a large cauldron, and finely crafted drinking vessels. These items reflect the chieftain's status and the belief in an afterlife where such luxuries would be needed.

SIGNIFICANT ARTIFACTS

The material culture of the Celts is replete with artifacts that provide a window into their mythological and religious world. These objects, ranging from everyday items to ceremonial treasures, are often adorned with symbolic motifs and intricate designs.

The Gundestrup Cauldron

One of the most famous artifacts associated with Celtic mythology is the Gundestrup Cauldron. Discovered in a peat bog in Denmark in 1891, this silver cauldron dates to the 1st or 2nd century BC and is believed to have been made by Thracian craftsmen for a Celtic patron. The cauldron is decorated with elaborate reliefs depicting various deities, animals, and mythological scenes. The central figure on one of the panels is often identified as Cernunnos, the horned god of nature and fertility. He is depicted holding a torc (a symbol of nobility) and a serpent, surrounded by animals such as deer and wolves. Other panels show scenes of ritual sacrifice, warriors, and deities, providing a vivid representation of Celtic religious and mythological beliefs.

The Battersea Shield

The Battersea Shield, discovered in the River Thames in London in 1857, is another remarkable example of Celtic craftsmanship. Dating to the 1st century BC, this bronze shield is decorated with intricate repoussé work, featuring swirling patterns and inlaid enamel. The shield is believed to have been a votive offering, possibly dedicated to a river deity. The design of the Battersea Shield reflects the Celts' mastery of metalworking and their use of symbolic motifs. The swirling patterns are reminiscent of the La Tène style, while the presence of red enamel may symbolize blood and life force, underscoring the shield's ritual significance.

The Turoe Stone

The Turoe Stone, located in County Galway, Ireland, is a striking example of Celtic stone carving. This granite boulder, dating to the 1st century BC, is covered with intricate La Tène-style carvings, including spirals, triskeles, and interlacing patterns. The stone is believed to have been a ceremonial or boundary marker, possibly associated with the worship of local deities. The Turoe Stone's elaborate carvings highlight the Celts' skill in working with stone and their use of art to convey spiritual and mythological themes. The motifs on the stone are thought to represent the cyclical nature of life and the interconnectedness of the natural and supernatural worlds.

Above: The Battersea Shield, by chance dredged from the Thames in 1857 during construction work for the old Chelsea Bridge. It can be seen in The British Museum; **Below:** The Gundestrup Cauldron, discovered in a peat bog in northern Denmark in 1891. It was found in pieces and has been reconstituted to its original form—*See over for more images*

RITUAL OBJECTS AND VOTIVE OFFERINGS

Ritual objects and votive offerings are a significant aspect of Celtic material culture, reflecting the importance of religious practices and the veneration of deities. These objects, often deposited in rivers, lakes, and other sacred sites, were intended to appease the gods and ensure their favor.

The Llyn Cerrig Bach Hoard

The Llyn Cerrig Bach Hoard, discovered in a lake on the island of Anglesey, Wales, is one of the most important collections of Celtic votive offerings. Dating from the 2nd century BC to the 1st century AD, the hoard includes weapons, tools, chariot fittings, and personal ornaments. The items were deliberately broken before being deposited, a practice believed to release their spiritual essence for the gods. The Llyn Cerrig Bach Hoard provides valuable insights into the Celts' ritual practices and their belief in the power of offerings to communicate with the divine. The presence of high-status items in the hoard suggests that the offerings were made by elite members of society, underscoring the communal nature of Celtic religious practices.

Opposite, main image: a dramatically-lit close-up of the Gundestrup Cauldron. It's believed to be a likeness of the Dagda, a major Celtic deity; **Opposite, below:** an intricately-worked bronze plaque from the Llyn Cerrig Bach Hoard, discovered in 1942 in Llyn Cerrig Bach lake, on the Isle of Anglesey in North Wales. 150 pieces of Iron Age metalwork had been sunk into the lake as votive offerings; **Centerfold:** The Turoe Stone, a National Monument of Ireland, is located in Bullaun, County Galway, and dates back to 100 BC; **Above:** The Golden Boat, and **Left:** the Golden Torc, both part of the Broighter Hoard, discovered in County Derry in 1896 by farmers plowing land reclaimed from Lough Foyle. It can be seen in the National Museum of Ireland in Dublin; **Below:** The intricate silverwork of an inside panel of the Gundestrup Cauldron

The Broighter Hoard

The Broighter Hoard, discovered in County Derry, Northern Ireland, is another significant collection of Celtic artifacts. Dating to the 1st century BC, the Broighter Hoard includes a gold torc, a miniature boat, and various other gold objects. The items are believed to have been votive offerings, possibly dedicated to a water deity. The craftsmanship is exceptional, with the gold torc and boat displaying intricate designs and fine detailing. The hoard reflects the Celts' reverence for water as a sacred element, and their use of precious materials to honor their deities.

RITUALS AND FESTIVALS

Celtic culture was deeply intertwined with the cycles of nature and the agricultural calendar, reflected in the festivals, holidays, and rituals celebrated by the ancient Celts.

Above: The festival of Samhain marked the end of the harvest, and the arrival of winter—the "dark half" of the annual cycle; **Top left:** Imbolc rituals were also signified by tribal bonfires; **Top right:** Jack O' Lanterns were originally made from turnips, rather than pumpkins, but it's the origin of the Christian concept of Halloween. Courtesy of the Seed Company

These events were not only times of communal gathering and celebration but also held profound spiritual significance, marking the transitions of the seasons and honoring the deities and spirits that governed the natural world. This exploration delves into the major Celtic festivals, the associated rituals, and their enduring legacy in modern times.

THE CELTIC CALENDAR

The Celtic year was divided into two main halves: the light half and the dark half. This division was marked by four major festivals, each corresponding to a significant point in the agricultural and solar calendar. These festivals are **Samhain**, **Imbolc**, **Beltane**, and **Lughnasadh**, each with its own unique customs and rituals.

Samhain

Samhain, celebrated from October 31st to November 1st, marks the end of the harvest season and the beginning of the dark half of the year. It is one of the most important festivals in the Celtic calendar, often considered the Celtic New Year. Samhain is a time when the veil between the mortal world and the Otherworld is believed to be at its thinnest, allowing spirits and supernatural beings to cross over. Samhain rituals often involved lighting bonfires, which were believed to have protective and cleansing properties.

THE CELTIC WORLD
Feast of Imbolc, Italy

The four main Celtic seasonal festivals which span the solar year have been long celebrated in Ireland, though today they have been taken up by small groups across Europe. A Feast of Imbolc was celebrated in Axa Briga Park, Italy, in 2019. Imbolc, or *Imbolg*, is a traditional Gaelic festival marking the beginning of spring, with its traditional date of 1 February—halfway between the winter solstice and the spring equinox. Its traditions were widely observed throughout Ireland, Scotland and the Isle of Man.

Above left and right: A Celtic Feast of Imbolc took place in Axa Briga Park, Settimo Rottaro, Italy in 2019; **Below:** A modern fantasy impression of the Celtic deity Brigid, a goddess of fertility, healing, and poetry, and closely associated with the festival of Imbolc. (See pages 42–43.)

People would gather around these fires to offer sacrifices of crops and animals to appease the gods and spirits. The flames were also used to guide the souls of the dead back to the Otherworld. Another common practice was the carving of turnips (later pumpkins) into lanterns, known as "Jack O' Lanterns," to ward off evil spirits. People would also dress in costumes and masks, a tradition that has evolved into modern Halloween, to disguise themselves from wandering spirits. Feasting and storytelling were central to Samhain celebrations, with tales of ancestors, heroes, and gods being recounted. Divination rituals, such as scrying and casting lots, were also performed to gain insights into the future.

Imbolc

Imbolc, celebrated on February 1st, marks the midpoint between the winter solstice and the spring equinox. It is a festival of light and purification, heralding the return of the sun and the beginning of the agricultural year. Imbolc is closely associated with the goddess Brigid, a deity of fertility, healing, and poetry. Imbolc rituals often involved the lighting of candles and fires to symbolize the increasing strength of the sun. Homes and hearths were cleaned and purified, and offerings of milk and butter were made to Brigid. Crosses made of rushes or straw, known as Brigid's crosses, were crafted and placed in homes for protection and blessings. Wells and springs, sacred to Brigid, were visited, and water was drawn for its healing properties. People would also leave strips of cloth, known as clooties, tied to trees near these wells, believing that the goddess would bless them with health and prosperity. Feasting and poetry recitals were integral to Imbolc celebrations, honoring Brigid's role as a patron of the arts. The festival was a time for community bonding and the reaffirmation of social ties.

Top: A modern carved stone frieze of Belenus; **Above:** Belenus, a deity of light and fire. A modern fantasy depiction; **Below:** Another modern fantasy illustration, this one of Lugh—a deity also associated by the Celts with light, as well as skill and craftsmanship, and celebrated during the Lughnasadh, the beginning of the harvest season.

Beltane

Beltane, celebrated on May 1st, marks the beginning of the light half of the year and the arrival of summer. It is a festival of fertility, growth, and renewal, celebrating the blossoming of nature and the return of life. Beltane is associated with the god Belenus, a deity of light and fire. Beltane rituals prominently feature the lighting of bonfires, known as Beltane fires, which were believed to have protective and purifying powers. Cattle were driven between two fires to ensure their health and fertility for the coming year. People would leap over the flames or pass through the smoke for blessings and protection. Maypoles, adorned with ribbons and flowers, were erected as symbols of fertility and the union of the earth and sky. Dancing around the maypole was a central activity, with participants weaving intricate patterns with the ribbons. Another important custom was the gathering of May dew, which was believed to have magical properties. People would wash their faces with the dew to enhance beauty and health. Flowers and greenery were collected to decorate homes and altars, celebrating the abundance of nature.

Lughnasadh

Lughnasadh, celebrated on August 1st, marks the beginning of the harvest season and honors the god Lugh, a deity of light, skill, and craftsmanship. The festival is named after Lugh and is a time of thanksgiving for the first fruits of the harvest. Lughnasadh rituals often involved the reaping of the first grains and the baking of the first bread from the new harvest. Offerings of bread, fruits, and grains were made to Lugh and other deities to ensure a bountiful harvest. Feasting and communal meals were central to the celebrations, with people sharing the fruits of their labor. Athletic contests and games, known as the Tailteann Games, were held in honor of Lugh's foster mother, Tailtiu, who is said to have died from exhaustion after clearing the land for agriculture. These games included feats of strength, horse racing, and other competitions, celebrating physical prowess and skill. Craft fairs and markets were also common during Lughnasadh, reflecting Lugh's association with craftsmanship and trade. People would gather to exchange goods, showcase their talents, and strengthen community bonds.

OTHER FESTIVALS AND RITUALS

In addition to the four major festivals, the Celts celebrated various other holidays and rituals that marked important points in the agricultural and solar calendar.

Winter Solstice (*Alban Arthan*)

The winter solstice, known as *Alban Arthan* in Welsh tradition, marks the longest night of the year and the rebirth of the Sun. Celebrations often involved the lighting of fires and candles to symbolize the return of light. Yule logs, decorated with holly and ivy, were burned to bring warmth and light into the home.

Summer Solstice (*Alban Hefin*)

The summer solstice, known as *Alban Hefin*, marks the longest day of the year and the height of the sun's power. Celebrations included bonfires, feasting, and dancing, honoring the sun's life-giving energy. It was a time for gathering herbs, believed to be at their most potent, and performing rituals for health and prosperity.

Left: The winter solstice, *Alban Arthan* in the old Welsh tradition, marking the shortest day, and the rebirth of the Sun. For the Celts of Northern Europe, the sun was seen in the lowest part of the sky, and set quickly; **Below:** The entrance to the 5,000 year-old Newgrange Tumulus in County Meath, Ireland, one of three major burial sites at the Brú na Bóinne complex in the Boyne River valley, some 40 km north of Dublin; **Bottom:** Nether Largie South Cairn, one of several Neolithic cairns in Kilmartin Glen, Argyll & Bute, Scotland.

Rituals of Life and Death

Celtic rituals obviously also encompassed important life events such as births, marriages, and deaths. Birth rituals often involved the blessing of the newborn with water and the invocation of protective deities. Marriage ceremonies, known as handfastings, included the binding of the couple's hands with a cord, symbolizing their union. Funerary rituals were elaborate, reflecting the belief in an afterlife and the journey of the soul to the Otherworld. Burial mounds, or tumuli, were constructed, and grave goods were placed with the deceased to aid them in the afterlife. Samhain was a particularly important time for honoring the dead, with rituals to ensure their peaceful passage and to seek their guidance.

IRISH MYTHOLOGY

1

The vibrant tapestry of Irish mythology forms a cornerstone of Celtic mythology. Rooted in oral tradition but preserved through centuries of history, these ancient stories of mortal heroes, supernatural beings, and mysterious other worlds offer a window into the beliefs and culture of ancient Ireland

Opposite: A mystical woodland scene in Glenveagh National Park, Donegal

INTRODUCTION

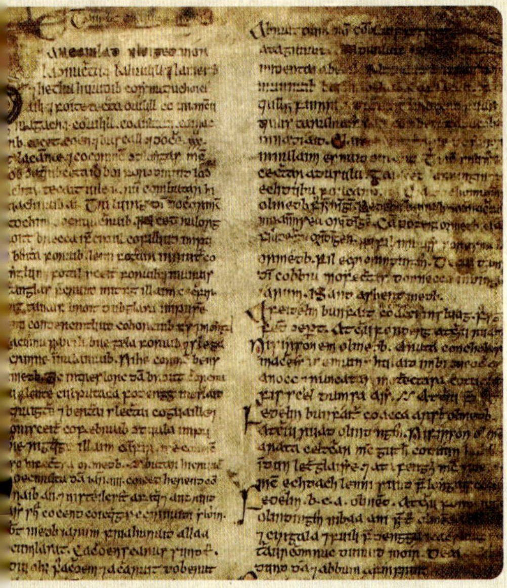

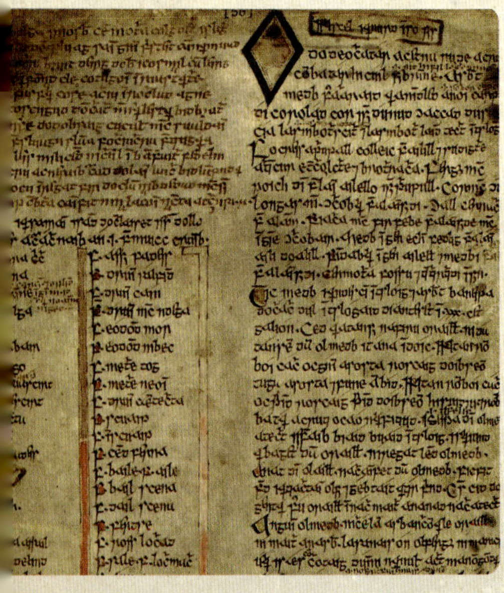

Above: Detail of pages from *Lebor na hUidre* (*Book of the Dun Cow*)—a primary source of Irish mythology. Courtesy of the Royal Irish Academy Library, Dublin.

These ancient tales, this body of lore, passed down through generations via oral tradition and later transcribed by medieval monks, offer profound insights into the beliefs, values, and cultural identity of the early Irish people. The mythology is not only a reflection of the spiritual and social fabric of ancient Ireland but also serves as an invaluable repository of the island's pre-Christian heritage.

HISTORICAL CONTEXT AND SOURCES

Irish mythology makes up the bulk of Celtic mythology as a whole, as most of the myths and legends that were recorded in writing and passed down over the centuries are Irish in origin. The primary sources of Irish mythology are medieval manuscripts, most notably the *Lebor na hUidre* (*Book of the Dun Cow*), the *Book of Leinster*, and *The Book of Glendalough.* These texts, written in Old and Middle Irish, were compiled by Christian monks who sought to preserve the oral traditions of their pagan ancestors. Despite the Christian bias, the manuscripts retain a wealth of pre-Christian themes and characters, providing a window into the ancient Celtic worldview.

MYTHOLOGICAL CYCLES

Irish mythology is traditionally divided into four major chronological cycles: the Mythological Cycle, the Ulster Cycle, the Fenian Cycle, and the Historical Cycle. Each cycle encompasses a distinct set of narratives and characters, reflecting different aspects of Irish life and belief.

The Mythological Cycle

The Mythological Cycle, also known as the Cycle of the Gods, is the oldest and most enigmatic of the four. It centers on the Tuatha Dé Danann, a race of supernatural beings who are often depicted as gods and goddesses and pave the way for later depictions of fairies in Irish folklore.
Key texts in this cycle include the *Lebor Gabála Érenn* (*The Book of Invasions*), which recounts the successive invasions and settlements of Ireland, culminating in the arrival of the Tuatha Dé Danann. Prominent figures in this cycle include Dagda, the chief god; Brigid, the goddess of healing and poetry; and Lugh, the god of light and craftsmanship.

The Ulster Cycle

The Ulster Cycle, also known as the Red Branch Cycle, is a collection of heroic tales set in the province of Ulster. These stories are characterized by their focus on warrior culture and the exploits of legendary heroes. The central figure of this cycle is Cú Chulainn, a demigod and warrior whose feats and tragic fate are detailed in the epic *Táin Bó Cúailnge* (*The Cattle Raid of Cooley*). Other notable characters include Conchobar mac Nessa, the king of Ulster, and Queen Medb of Connacht, a formidable antagonist.

The Fenian Cycle

The Fenian Cycle, or the Ossianic Cycle, revolves around the adventures of Fionn

mac Cumhaill (Finn MacCool) and his band of warriors, the Fianna. These tales, set in a more pastoral and romanticized Ireland, emphasize themes of loyalty, bravery, and the bond between man and nature. The *Acallam na Senórach* (The *Colloquy of the Ancients*) is a key text in this cycle, featuring dialogues between the aged warriors of the Fianna and Saint Patrick. Fionn's son, Oisín, is also a prominent figure, known for his poetic prowess and his journey to the otherworldly land of Tír na nÓg.

The Historical Cycle

The Historical Cycle, also referred to as the Cycle of the Kings, blends myth and history, chronicling the deeds of Ireland's legendary and semi-historical kings. This cycle includes tales of figures such as Cormac mac Airt, Niall of the Nine Hostages, and Brian Boru. While these stories often contain fantastical elements, they are rooted in the historical and genealogical traditions of medieval Ireland.

THEMES AND MOTIFS

Irish mythology is replete with recurring themes and motifs that reflect the values and concerns of ancient Irish society. Central to these narratives is the concept of sovereignty, often personified as a goddess who bestows kingship upon a worthy ruler. The theme of the hero's journey, marked by trials, quests, and transformations, is also prevalent, illustrating the virtues of courage, honor, and resilience. The otherworld, a realm inhabited by gods, spirits, and the dead, plays a significant role in Irish mythology. This mystical land, accessible through sacred sites, dreams, or death, is depicted as both a place of peril and paradise. The interplay between the mortal world and the otherworld underscores the belief in the permeability of boundaries between the natural and supernatural realms.

Above: Inside the Knowth tumulus—in the Celtic belief system, it's the beginning of the Otherworld; **Main image, top:** Aerial view of the great Knowth tumulus, part of the major Brú na Bóinne (Valley of the Boyne) complex in County Meath, Ireland, around 40km north of Dublin. The site is one of the world's most important prehistoric landscapes and includes the three large sacred passage graves of Knowth, Newgrange and Dowth, as well as some ninety additional monuments. Since 1993, a World Heritage Site, designated by UNESCO.

DEITIES

The Tuatha Dé Danann, translated as "the People of the Goddess Danu," are a supernatural race in Irish mythology, known for their magical abilities, wisdom, and artistic skills.

Above: "Manannán put a powerful enchantment on the shield..." An illustration by Beatrice Elvery from *Heroes of the Dawn* by Violet Russell, 1914; **Top:** "Deep in the moonlit forest, the God Dagda calls his magic harp to him." An illustration by Stephen Reid, circa 1909

They are the pantheon of gods of ancient Irish mythology, although later sources recorded by Christian scholars tended to avoid referring to the Tuatha Dé Danann explicitly as deities. They are one of the most prominent and influential groups in the Mythological Cycle of Ireland, playing a central role in the island's legendary history and shaping its cultural identity.

Origins and Arrival in Ireland

According to the mythological accounts, the Tuatha Dé Danann descended from the goddess Danu, a maternal figure associated with fertility, abundance, and wisdom. Their origins are shrouded in mystery, with some stories suggesting that they came from the heavens or the northern islands of the world. In the *Lebor Gabála Érenn* (*The Book of Invasions*), an 11th-century text that recounts the mythical history of Ireland, the Tuatha Dé Danann are described as the fifth group to settle on the island. The Tuatha Dé Danann arrived in Ireland on dark clouds, landing on the mountain of *Sliabh an Iarainn* (the *Iron Mountain*) in the west of the country.

Battles and Reign in Ireland

Upon their arrival, the Tuatha Dé Danann faced opposition from the Fir Bolg, the previous inhabitants of Ireland. In the First Battle of Mag Tuired, the Tuatha Dé Danann, led by their king Nuada, defeated the Fir Bolg and established their rule over the island. However, Nuada lost his arm in the battle, and due to the Tuatha Dé Danann's belief that their king must be physically perfect, he was forced to relinquish his kingship to Bres, a half-Fomorian prince. Bres proved to be an oppressive ruler, and the Tuatha Dé Danann suffered under his reign. Nuada, having received a silver arm crafted by the physician Dian Cecht and the wright Creidhne, reclaimed his kingship. This led to the Second Battle of Mag Tuired, in which the Tuatha Dé Danann faced the Fomorians, a race of monstrous beings

who sought to conquer Ireland. In a fierce battle, the Tuatha Dé Danann, now led by the hero Lugh, defeated the Fomorians and secured their rule over Ireland. The Tuatha Dé Danann reigned over Ireland for many years, bringing prosperity and peace to the land. They were known for their wisdom, magical abilities, and artistic skills, and their reign was considered a golden age in Irish mythology.

Decline and Legacy

The reign of the Tuatha Dé Danann came to an end with the arrival of the Milesians, the final group to settle in Ireland according to the *Lebor Gabála Érenn*. In a series of battles, the Milesians, led by the brothers Eber Finn and Eremon, defeated the Tuatha Dé Danann and claimed the island for themselves. As part of the peace agreement, the Tuatha Dé Danann retreated to the Otherworld, the magical realm that existed alongside the mortal world. In the Otherworld, the Tuatha Dé Danann continued to influence the lives of mortals, often appearing in stories and legends as powerful beings who could help or hinder human endeavors. They were associated with the *sidhe*, the ancient mounds and burial sites that dotted the Irish landscape, and were believed to inhabit these places.

Above: The Milesians arriving in Ireland, by Stephen Reid, from *Myths and Legends of the Celtic Race*, 1910; **TOP:** *Riders of the Sidhe*, the Tuatha Dé Danann, by Scottish folklorist painter John Duncan, 1911

LUGH

Lugh, also known as *Lugh Lámhfhada* (Lugh of the Long Arm), is one of the most prominent gods in Irish mythology.

Above: A stone relief carving of a three-faced god from northeastern Gaul, believed to be Lugus, the Gaulish equivalent of Lugh. Discovered in Reims in 1852, now in the Musée St. Remi, in Reims; **Top, right:** Illustration by Maud Gonne for *The Coming of Lugh*, retold by Ella Young and published in 1909 by Maunsel & Co., Dublin

A member of the supernatural race known as the Tuatha Dé Danann, Lugh is a multi-talented figure associated with skill, crafts, the arts, and heroism. His influence extends across the Celtic world, with cognates in Welsh mythology (*Lleu Llaw Gyffes*) and Gaulish inscriptions (*Lugus*).

ORIGINS AND ASSOCIATIONS

Lugh's name is derived from the Proto-Celtic root *lug-*, meaning "oath" or "to swear," suggesting his role as a god of contracts and agreements. This etymology also connects him to the concept of kingship, as oaths were a crucial part of the relationship between a king and his subjects in Celtic society. Additionally, his epithet Lámhfhada ("of the long arm") may refer to his skill with weapons, particularly the spear, or to his far-reaching influence and authority. In Irish mythology, Lugh is associated with a wide range of attributes, including oaths, craftsmanship, the sun, sovereignty, and heroism.

MYTHOLOGICAL NARRATIVES

Lugh features prominently in several key stories within the Irish mythological cycle:

The Coming of Lugh

In the tale of Lugh's arrival at the court of King Nuada of the Tuatha Dé Danann, the god is initially denied entry by the gatekeeper, who informs him that only those with a specific skill or talent are allowed to join the court. Lugh proceeds to list his many abilities, including his mastery of carpentry, blacksmithing, poetry, and warfare. Impressed by his diverse talents, Nuada welcomes Lugh into his court, recognizing him as a valuable addition to the Tuatha Dé Danann.

The Battle of Mag Tuired

Lugh plays a central role in the Second Battle of Mag Tuired, in which the Tuatha Dé Danann face off against their enemies, the Fomorians. Prior to the battle, Lugh visits the Fomorian camp disguised as a young boy and tricks them into revealing their weaknesses. Armed with this knowledge, he leads the Tuatha Dé Danann to victory, personally slaying the Fomorian leader Balor of the Evil Eye, who happens to be his grandfather. This decisive battle establishes Lugh as a hero and savior of his people.

Lugh and Cú Chulainn

In the Ulster Cycle of Irish mythology, Lugh is portrayed as the divine father of the hero Cú Chulainn. He appears to Cú Chulainn in visions and dreams, offering guidance and support throughout the hero's adventures. This connection further emphasizes Lugh's role as a patron of heroes and his influence on the mortal world.

FESTIVALS AND WORSHIP

Lugh is associated with the Lughnasadh festival, which marks the beginning of the harvest season. Celebrated on August 1st, Lughnasadh is one of the four main festivals in the Celtic calendar, along with Samhain, Imbolc, and Beltane. The festival's name, derived from Lugh's own name, points to his significance in Celtic religious practices. Archaeological evidence suggests that Lugh was worshipped at various sites across the Celtic world, including Lugdunum (modern-day Lyon, France) and the Lugh-associated temple at Peñalba de Villastar in Spain. These widespread traces of his cult attest to his importance and influence in Celtic religion.

Top, main image: A modern fantasy illustration of Lugh, courtesy of Paganista; **Above:** An AI-generated image of Lugh, courtesy of Nightcafe Studio

THE DAGDA

The Dagda, whose name means "the good god," is a father-figure and ruler in the pantheon of Irish mythology. As a chief of the Tuatha Dé Danann, he embodies the qualities of strength, wisdom, magic, and fertility.

Top: A modern impression of the Dagda as "the good god," and father figure of the Tuatha Dé Danann; **Above:** The Dagda serenely contemplates the idyllic Irish countryside with his staff (here depicted as a great axe), his bottomless cauldron, and magic harp, which is able to fly to him when commanded

The Dagda's influence permeates the mythological landscape, shaping the tales of gods and heroes alike.

ATTRIBUTES AND POSSESSIONS

Known for his immense strength and stature, the Dagda is often depicted as a large, bearded man wearing a hooded cloak and carrying a magical club and cauldron. His club, known as the *lorg mór* or great staff, has the power to slay nine men with a single blow, while his cauldron, the *coire ansic* or the undry cauldron, is said to be bottomless, providing an endless supply of food. In addition to these iconic possessions, the Dagda is associated with the seasons, agriculture, and fertility. His cauldron symbolizes the abundance of the harvest and the nourishment of the land. As a god of the earth and its bounty, the Dagda is closely linked to the cycles of nature and the well-being of his people. His name was invoked during the feast of Samhain—the beginning of the dark half of the year—to ensure that the soul spirits of the dead would not cross the veil and return to trouble the tribe.

MYTHOLOGICAL TALES

The Dagda appears in numerous stories throughout Irish mythology, often playing a central role in the affairs of the Tuatha Dé Danann. In the tale of the Second

Battle of Mag Tuired, the Dagda forms an alliance with the Mórrígan, a powerful goddess of war and fate. Together, they visit the Fomorian camp, where the Dagda tricks the enemy into revealing their weaknesses, aiding in the Tuatha Dé Danann's ultimate victory. Another notable story involving the Dagda is his encounter with the goddess Boann. According to the tale, Boann, the wife of Nechtan, visits the Dagda's home while her husband is away. The two engage in a tryst, which results in the conception of Aengus, the god of love and youth. To hide their affair, the Dagda causes the sun to stand still for nine months, allowing Boann to give birth to Aengus in a single day.

The Dagda and the Otherworld

As a god of abundance and fertility, the Dagda is closely associated with the Otherworld, the realm of the gods and the dead in Irish mythology. His cauldron, which provides endless sustenance, is reminiscent of the regenerative powers of the Otherworld. The Dagda's role as a mediator between the world of mortals and the divine is further emphasized by his ability to move freely between these realms. In some tales, the Dagda is portrayed as the ruler of the Otherworld, presiding over the feast of eternal plenty at his great hall. This association with the afterlife and the cycle of death and rebirth underscores the Dagda's significance as a god of renewal and transformation.

GEOGRAPHICAL ASSOCIATIONS

The Dagda is associated with several important sites of Irish mythology: The Hill of Uisneach (in English, Ushnagh), in County Westmeath, a prehistoric ceremonial site consisting of many earthworks, tombs and standing stones, and reputedly the burial site of Dagda and Lugh—amongst other deities of the Tuatha Dé Danann. The Dagda is also said to dwell in Newgrange, part of the Brú na Bóinne ancient monument complex, and his magical club is said to be buried on the Hill of Tara, in County Meath, the seat of the High Kings of Ireland.

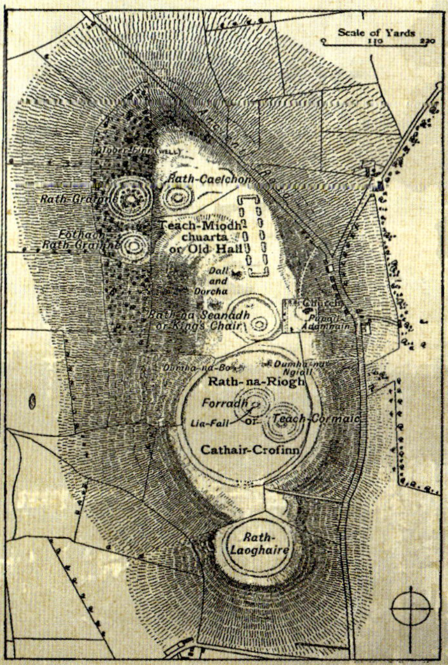

Top, left: The likeness of the Dagda on the Gundestrup Cauldron (see pages 22–25); **Top, right:** Modern, retro-style painting of the Dagda; **Above:** "The Plan of Tara," based on a survey of the site and historical records, drawn by William Wakeman and published in *Wakeman's Handbook of Irish Antiquities*, 1903

THE MORRIGAN

The Morrigan, whose name translates to "Great Queen" or "Phantom Queen," is a complex and multifaceted goddess in Irish mythology. Often depicted as a triple goddess, the Morrigan encompasses the identities of Badb, Macha, and Nemain, each representing different aspects of her power and influence.

Above, and **Top, right:** Digitally-generated modern fantasy interpretations of the Morrigan, the triple goddess of war, fate and sovereignty, courtesy Luna Moonfall (top) and Old World Gods; **Opposite:** *The goddess Macha curses the Men of Ulster.* Illustration by Stephen Reid, from Eleanor Hull's *Cuchulain The Hound of Ulster*, Harrap, London, 1909

As a goddess of war, fate, and sovereignty, the Morrigan plays a crucial role in the tales of gods and heroes, shaping the destinies of those who cross her path. One of the most striking aspects of the Morrigan is her ability to transform and shape-shift, taking on various forms to influence the course of events. This transformative power is not limited to physical form; the Morrigan also embodies the transformative power of war, death, and rebirth.

In her role as a goddess of war, the Morrigan presides over the destruction and chaos of the battlefield, but she is also a catalyst for change and renewal. Through the crucible of conflict, the Morrigan brings about the transformation of individuals, societies, and even the land itself.

ASPECTS AND ASSOCIATIONS

The Morrigan's three main aspects, Badb, Macha, and Nemain, embody different facets of her divine nature:

Badb: Associated with battle, prophecy, and death, Badb is often portrayed as a harbinger of death and destruction. She is known to take the form of a crow or raven, flying over battlefields and influencing the outcome of conflicts.

Macha: Linked to sovereignty, fertility, and the land, Macha is sometimes depicted as a horse goddess. In one tale, she races against the king's horses while pregnant, giving birth at the finish line and cursing the men of Ulster to experience labor pains in times of crisis.

Nemain: Connected to panic, frenzy, and the chaos of battle, Nemain is said to instill fear and confusion in the hearts of warriors. Her presence on the battlefield is thought to turn the tide of war and bring about decisive victories.

The Morrigan and Cú Chulainn

The Morrigan plays a significant role in

the tales of the Ulster Cycle, particularly in the story of the hero Cú Chulainn. In the *Táin Bó Cúailnge, (The Cattle Raid of Cooley)*, the Morrigan appears to Cú Chulainn as a beautiful woman, offering him her love and aid in battle. When the hero rejects her advances, the Morrigan vows to hinder his efforts during the raid. Throughout the tale, the Morrigan takes on various forms, including that of an eel, a wolf, and a heifer, to challenge and obstruct Cú Chulainn. In the end, the hero is forced to recognize the Morrigan's power and accepts her help, leading to his victory in the battle.

The Morrigan and Prophecy

In addition to her roles in battle and sovereignty, the Morrigan is associated with prophecy and the foretelling of doom. In the tale of the Battle of Allen, the Morrigan appears to the legendary queen Medb, foretelling the destruction of her army and the death of her allies.

The Morrigan in Art and Literature

The Morrigan has captured the imagination of artists and writers for centuries, inspiring numerous depictions in literature, art, and popular culture. In medieval Irish literature, the Morrigan appears in stories where her complex nature and influence on the lives of heroes and kings are explored. In modern times, the Morrigan continues to be a popular figure in fantasy literature, comics, and video games.

BRIGID

Brigid, also known as Brigit or Bríg, is associated with spring, fertility, healing, poetry, and smithcraft. Her name is derived from the Proto-Celtic *Brigantī*, meaning "the exalted one."

Brigid is often portrayed as the daughter of the Dagda, a chief god of the Tuatha Dé Danann. In some tales, she is also associated with the poet Amergin and the physician Dian Cecht, reflecting her roles as a goddess of poetry and healing. Brigid is closely linked to the festival of Imbolc, celebrated on February 1st, which marks the beginning of spring. This festival was associated with the lactation of ewes, signifying Brigid's role as a goddess of fertility and abundance.

SYMBOLISM AND ICONOGRAPHY

Brigid is often depicted with symbols of spring and fertility, such as flowers, lambs, and milk. She is also associated with the arts, particularly poetry and metalworking. In some representations, she is shown holding a flame or a cross made of rushes, known as Brigid's cross.

MYTHOLOGICAL TALES

One of the most well-known stories involving Brigid is her association with perpetual, sacred flames. She is said to have established a sanctuary at Kildare, where a group of nuns tended an eternal flame in her honor. This tradition continued until the 16th century. Brigid is also credited with the invention of keening, a traditional Irish form of vocal lament for the dead. According to legend, she first keened when her son Ruadán died.

CHRISTIAN SYNCRETISM

With the arrival of Christianity in Ireland, the goddess Brigid was syncretized with Saint Brigid of Kildare, who founded a monastery in the 5th century. Many of the goddess's attributes, such as her association with sacred flames and healing, were transferred to the saint. This syncretism allowed for the preservation of pre-Christian traditions within the new religious context.

COMPARATIVE MYTHOLOGY

Brigid has parallels in other Celtic mythologies. In Welsh mythology, she is cognate with the goddess Brigantia, who was worshipped by the Brigantes tribe in northern Britain. In Gaulish mythology, she is associated with the goddess Brigindo, whose name also means "the exalted one."

Inset opposite: Brigid's crosses are still a tradition in Ireland, though now syncretized with Christianity. There are several variations of pattern, and include three-armed constructions too; **Opposite: left,** and **top right,** and **this page, top left:** The concept of Brigid, the Celtic goddess of spring, fertility and poetry, allows much latitude for modern fantasy expression, as in these seductive images; **Right:** Although adorned with halo, indicating the Christian Saint Brigid, this commercially available interior decor print is sold as her earlier Celtic incarnation

DANU

Danu is an important—if enigmatic—mother goddess in Irish mythology. She is believed to be the ancestor of the Tuatha Dé Danann ("People of the Goddess Danu"), a supernatural race that makes up the pantheon of Irish mythology.

Above: Danu, the ancestor of the Tuatha Dé Danann. Fantasy art courtesy of Irishhistory.com

While there are no stories or myths that directly feature Danu as a character, her influence and legacy are seen through her divine children. The Tuatha Dé Danann are depicted as god-like figures with supernatural abilities who engage in battles, romances, and adventures throughout the Irish mythological cycles.

As a mother goddess, Danu's role seems to have been as an ancestral figure of divine origins rather than an active participant in myths. She likely represented the earth, fertility, wisdom, and the primal forces of nature. Her name is thought to originate from the Proto-Indo-European root word meaning "waters" or "to flow," connecting her to rivers and the life-giving power of water. While Danu does not appear directly in any surviving tales, her importance is clear from the frequent references to the Tuatha Dé Danann. As their divine ancestor, she is the source of their supernatural power and wisdom. In this way, Danu's influence permeates Irish mythology even in her absence.

The Celts venerated mother goddesses as guardians of the land, nature, and their people. Danu likely served such a function as a protective, generative force watching over her divine children. Through the Tuatha Dé Danann, she is the ultimate source of the gifts of civilization -

agriculture, crafts, magic, and knowledge. In modern times, Danu continues to be an important figure in Celtic neopaganism and goddess spirituality movements. She is often revered as a symbol of the earth mother, female empowerment, and the sacredness of nature. While details about her original worship and attributes are scarce, Danu's legacy and impact on Irish mythology are undeniable.

Above: Danu, the mother goddess of Irish mythology. AI-generated art by Nightcafe Studio

AENGUS

Aengus, also known as Aengus Óg or Angus Mac Óg, is the youthful god of love, beauty, and poetry in Irish mythology.

Above: The beauty of Aengus was said to be so great that four birds would circle his head, singing sweet melodies that could lull anyone to sleep; **Opposite:** *Angus Óg, God of Love and Courtesy, Putting a Spell of Summer Calm on the Sea*, oil on canvas, by John Duncan, the Scottish folklorist painter, circa 1905-8. Courtesy National Galleries of Scotland

The son of the Dagda and the river goddess Boann, Aengus embodies the passion and exuberance of youth, as well as the transformative power of love.

Birth and Early Life

The story of Aengus's birth is a tale of magic and deception. His mother, Boann, was married to Nechtan, but she had an affair with the Dagda. To conceal their tryst and the resulting pregnancy, the Dagda caused the sun to stand still for nine months, allowing Boann to give birth to Aengus in a single day. Raised in secrecy, Aengus grew into a handsome and charming young man, beloved by all who knew him. His beauty was said to be so great that four birds would circle his head, singing sweet melodies that could lull anyone to sleep.

Aengus and the Brú na Bóinne

Aengus is closely associated with the Brú na Bóinne, a complex of Neolithic monuments in County Meath, Ireland. The most famous of these monuments is Newgrange, a passage tomb that is aligned with the rising sun on the winter solstice. According to legend, Aengus tricked his father, the Dagda, into giving him the Brú na Bóinne. Aengus asked to borrow the site for a day and a night, but when the Dagda returned to reclaim it, Aengus argued that all of eternity is made up of days and nights, thus making the Brú na Bóinne his forever.

Aengus and the Poetic Arts

As a god of poetry and inspiration, Aengus was closely associated with the bardic tradition in Celtic society. Poets and bards would invoke his name and seek his favor in their craft, believing that he could bestow upon them the gift of eloquence and creative vision. In some tales, Aengus is portrayed as a skilled musician, playing enchanting melodies on his harp that could soothe the hearts of all who heard them. This connection to music and poetry underscores his role as a patron of the arts and a source of artistic inspiration.

MODERN INTERPRETATIONS AND INFLUENCE

Today, Aengus remains an important figure in Celtic spirituality and popular culture. In modern Pagan and Wiccan practices, Aengus is often invoked as a patron of love, creativity, and inspiration. Beyond the realm of spirituality, Aengus has also inspired countless works of art, literature, and music.

As with many Celtic deities, Cernunnos is an enigmatic and complex figure, sometimes depicted as a horned god associated with the hunt—but also with fertility and nature.

Above: Cernunnos on the Pillar of the Boatmen, courtesy of the Museum of the Middle Ages, Paris France; **Top:** Fantasy interpretation of Cernunnos from Old World Gods

While there are limited written records about Cernunnos from the Celtic period, his image appears in numerous artifacts and artwork throughout the Celtic world, suggesting his importance in ancient Celtic religion and spirituality.

Some scholars have proposed that Cernunnos may have been a title or epithet rather than a proper name, applied to various horned deities worshipped by different Celtic tribes. This theory could explain the variations in his depictions and the lack of a single, cohesive mythology surrounding him.

DEPICTIONS AND ATTRIBUTES

Cernunnos is typically portrayed as a male figure with antlers or horns, often seated cross-legged and surrounded by animals. The most famous depiction of Cernunnos is found on the Gundestrup Cauldron, a silver ritual vessel discovered in Denmark dating back to the 1st or 2nd century BC. In this image, Cernunnos is shown holding a torc (a Celtic neck ring) in one hand and a serpent in the other, with various animals, including a stag, a boar, and a bull, surrounding him. Other depictions of Cernunnos show him with a ram-horned serpent, a symbol of fertility and regeneration. He is also sometimes portrayed with a cornucopia or a sack of coins, representing abundance and wealth.

ROLES AND ASSOCIATIONS

Cernunnos is often associated with nature, fertility, and abundance. His connection to the forest and the animals suggests that he may have been seen as a protector and provider, ensuring the well-being of both

CERNUNNOS

the natural world and the human realm. As a horned god, Cernunnos is also linked to the hunt and the cycle of life and death. The shedding and regrowth of his antlers may have symbolized the cyclical nature of existence and the regenerative power of the earth. Some scholars have suggested that Cernunnos may have been associated with the Otherworld and the realm of the dead. His presence on the Gundestrup Cauldron, which depicts scenes of ritual and sacrifice, could indicate his role as a *psychopomp*, guiding souls between the worlds of the living and the dead.

Cernunnos in Gallo-Roman Religion

During the period of Roman occupation in Gaul (modern-day France), Cernunnos appears to have been syncretized with Roman deities such as Mercury and Dis Pater. Gallo-Roman depictions of Cernunnos often show him with the attributes of these Roman gods, such as the caduceus (a staff with two intertwined snakes) associated with Mercury, or the cornucopia, a symbol of abundance and fertility.

Above: Cernunnos is honored on the Gundestrup Cauldron, one of the most important-ever archaeological finds of Celtic cultural artifacts. Discovered in a peat bog in northern Denmark in 1891, it was found in pieces and has been reconstituted to its original form (*see* pp17–19); **Top, left:** Cernunnos, pictured online by the Old World Gods site; **Top, right:** The Roman god Mercury is believed to have been a syncretization of Cernunnos, adapted by the Romans after they conquered Gaul and it became part of the Empire for several hundred years. This cast bronze statue of Mercury dates back to the 1st century AD. Courtesy of the Walters Art Museum, Mount Vernon, Baltimore. The Museum is free to visitors.

MANANNÁN

Manannán mac Lir, also known as Manann, is a prominent sea god in Irish mythology.

Top: Manannán, depicted in a coast landscape resembling the Giant's Causeway (see pages 112–113), courtesy of Old World Gods site; **Above:** The Golden Boat from the Broighter Hoard, believed to have been a votive offering to the sea god (see pages 22–25); **Opposite:** The statue of Manannán mac Lir at Gortmore viewing point on Binevenagh Mountain near Limavady, Co Londonderry. The work was sculpted by John Darren Sutton, who also worked on *the Game of Thrones* TV series. Picture courtesy of Eoin McConnell and Alamy.

As the god of the sea, Manannán is associated with the Otherworld, magic, and the mists that separate the mortal realm from the divine. His influence extends beyond Ireland, with parallels in Welsh and Manx mythology, making him a significant figure in the broader context of Celtic religion and spirituality.

ATTRIBUTES AND POSSESSIONS

As a sea god, Manannán is closely associated with the ocean, the weather, and the mists that separate the mortal world from the Otherworld. He is often depicted as a powerful and benevolent deity, who protects sailors and guides them through the perils of the sea. Manannán is said to possess several magical items that aid him in his role as a divine guardian—and occasional trickster. These include:

Scuabtuinne: A magical boat that can navigate without oars and travel swiftly across the sea;

Fragarach: A powerful sword that can cut through any armor and from which no one can escape;

Féth fíada: A magical cloak that can render the wearer invisible and transport them across great distances;

Crane Bag: A treasure bag that contains various magical items and is said to be made from the skin of Aoife, a woman who was transformed into a crane by Manannán.

Manannán and the Voyage of Bran

In the "Voyage of Bran," an early Irish tale, Manannán appears as a guide and protector to the mortal hero Bran mac Febail. Bran, enticed by the enchanting music of the Otherworld, sets out on a journey across the sea. Manannán appears to Bran and his crew, offering them guidance and protection as they navigate the perils of the ocean and the mysterious islands they encounter.

Manannán and Cormac mac Airt

In the tale of "Manannan at Play," the sea god visits the legendary Irish king Cormac mac Airt in disguise and engages him in a game of chess. During the game, Manannán reveals his true identity and imparts wisdom and knowledge to the king, highlighting his role as a divine mentor and source of inspiration.

Manannán and the Isle of Man

Manannán is closely associated with the Isle of Man, which bears his name. According to Manx tradition, Manannán was the first ruler of the island and protected it from invaders by shrouding it in mist. He is also said to have taught the inhabitants of the island the arts of navigation and weather forecasting, emphasizing his role as a benefactor and teacher.

EPONA

Epona, whose name means "Great Mare" in Gaulish, was a Celtic goddess associated with horses, fertility, and possibly the afterlife.

Above, left: Roman period altar piece to Epona, the horse goddess. Made of Sandstone. Köngen, South-western Germany, around AD 200. Courtesy of the Landesmuseum Württemberg, Stuttgart; **Above, right:** Replica of a Roman period altar consecration piece to Epona, in the Cambodunum Archaeological Park in Kempten, Schwaben, Southern Germany

Epona was widely worshipped throughout the Roman Empire between the 1st and 3rd centuries AD, particularly by the cavalry. Epona is notable for being one of the few Celtic deities to be adopted into the Roman pantheon without any changes to her attributes or iconography.

ETYMOLOGY AND ORIGINS

The name Epona is derived from the Gaulish word *epos* meaning "horse," combined with the augmentative suffix "-on" frequently found in the names of Gaulish deities. This clearly identifies her as a goddess intimately connected with horses. While her origins are uncertain, Epona was venerated by the Celtic peoples of Gaul, Britain, and the Danubian provinces. The oldest known reference to her is found in the *Satires of Juvenal* from the late 1st or early 2nd century AD. However, she likely has much older roots in Celtic religion prior to the Roman period.

ATTRIBUTES AND ICONOGRAPHY

In artwork, Epona is typically depicted as a woman seated sidesaddle on a horse, or surrounded by horses. Her attributes include a patera (a shallow dish used for offerings), a cornucopia (symbolizing abundance), keys, and ears of grain. These suggest a role as a goddess of fertility and prosperity in addition to her equine associations.

WORSHIP AND CULT

Epona was widely worshiped throughout the Celtic world, with evidence of her cult found in Britain, Gaul, and parts of the Iberian Peninsula. Her popularity was particularly strong among the equestrian classes, including cavalry soldiers, horse breeders, and those involved in the care and training of horses. The worship of Epona often involved the creation of small shrines or altars in stables and barns, where offerings and prayers were made to ensure the health and well-being of horses. Inscriptions and dedications to Epona have been found in numerous archaeological sites, attesting to the widespread nature of her cult. As Epona's popularity grew, her worship was adopted by the Roman military, particularly the auxiliary cavalry units recruited from Celtic regions. Roman soldiers spread her cult throughout the empire, leading to the establishment of temples and shrines dedicated to Epona in various provinces.

FUNERARY AND AFTERLIFE ASSOCIATIONS

Some scholars believe that in addition to her role as a horse and fertility goddess, Epona may have served a *psychopomp* function, guiding the souls of the dead to the afterlife. This is suggested by funerary monuments that depict her alongside the deceased.

Above: A third Roman period altar piece to Epona, this time discovered in Trieste, Italy, 1928; **Main image:** The Uffington White Horse, on the Berkshire Downs, England. It's situated close to the Iron Age Uffington Castle hillfort contours, which are of a similar geological appearance to Glastonbury Tor—King Arthur's "Isle of Avalon." Both are located close to the Ridgeway, an ancient track which has been used by travelers for at least 5,000 years.

FAIRIES

The *Aos Sí*, often translated as "fairies" or "people of the mounds," are a significant part of Irish mythology and folklore.

Above: *The Fairies' Favourite.* Fairies feeding a squirrel with nuts, a drawing in the style of Richard Dadd by J. Arnold, and engraved on wood by Henry Lynton, circa 1870; **Top right:** Fairies—the 19th-century vision; **Opposite, top left:** *Take the Fair Face of Woman, and Gently Suspending, With Butterflies, Flowers, and Jewels Attending, Thus Your Fairy is Made of Most Beautiful Things*, by Sophie Anderson, 1869, from a verse by Charles Ede; **Opposite, top right:** *Oberon, Titania and Puck with Fairies Dancing*, by William Blake, circa 1786. Watercolor and graphite on paper. A scene from Shakespeare's *A Midsummer Night's Dream*; **Opposite, center:** *The Fairies (Le Villi)*, by Bartolomeo Giuliano, circa 1866. Gallerie di Piazza Scala, Milano; **Opposite, bottom right:** *The Faerie Queene; The Quarrel of Oberon and Titania* by Joseph Paton, oil on canvas, 1849. Another depiction from *A Midsummer Night's Dream*.

These supernatural beings are believed to inhabit an unseen world parallel to our own, the Otherworld.

The term "Aos Sí" directly translates to "people of the sídhe" or "mounds," referring to the ancient burial mounds across Ireland, where these beings are thought to dwell. Revered and feared in equal measure, the Aos Sí are considered both protectors and, at times, punishers, embodying the mysterious and unpredictable forces of nature.

ORIGINS AND DESCRIPTION

The origins of the Aos Sí can be traced back to ancient Celtic beliefs about the natural world and its hidden powers. They are often regarded as descendants of the Tuatha Dé Danann, a race of god-like beings who inhabited Ireland before being displaced by the Milesians, the ancestors of the modern Irish. According to legend, the Tuatha Dé Danann retreated into the hills and mounds, becoming the Aos Sí. Over time, these beings transitioned from deities to spirits of the land, retaining their supernatural abilities but shifting in cultural perception to the status of fairies or lesser gods.

The Aos Sí are diverse in form and demeanor. They are usually depicted as ethereal beings, similar to humans but often more beautiful and otherworldly. Some accounts describe them as diminutive and delicate, while others portray them as of average human size or even larger. They can be benevolent or malevolent depending on their disposition and how they are treated by humans. Many tales depict them as possessing powers over life, fertility, and nature, and they are known to be capable of both great kindness and swift retribution.

Habitats and the Otherworld

The Aos Sí are believed to reside in the Otherworld, a mystical realm that exists alongside the human world but is accessible only through special means. The Otherworld is associated with natural features such as mounds, hollow hills, and forests. These features are thought to serve as portals between the mortal realm and the fairy world, linking the Aos Sí closely with the landscape of Ireland.

The mounds, known as "fairy forts," are often sites of ancient ringforts or burial sites from prehistoric times. People in Ireland still hold a certain reverence for these places, avoiding disturbances to avoid incurring the wrath of the fairies. The Aos Sí are believed to be especially active during certain times of the year, such as Samhain and Beltane, when the veil between the worlds is at its thinnest, allowing them to move freely between the two realms.

Characteristics and Behavior

The Aos Sí are known for their unpredictable nature. They can be benevolent, offering assistance and blessings to those who respect them, but they are also capable of causing harm to those who offend or disrespect their domain. Offerings of milk, butter, or other foodstuffs are traditionally left at doorways or near fairy mounds to appease them, reflecting a belief that maintaining a good relationship with the Aos Sí can bring protection and good fortune.

One of the key characteristics of the Aos Sí is their fierce guardianship of their realm. They do not tolerate incursions into their territory, and those who cut down fairy trees or interfere with their mounds often suffer misfortune or illness as a result. This has led to the preservation of many natural landmarks in Ireland, with people avoiding the disturbance of areas believed to be linked to the fairies. The Aos Sí are also known for their interactions with humans, often taking an interest in mortal affairs.

Stories of fairy abductions are common in Irish folklore, where individuals are lured or taken to the Otherworld, sometimes never to return. In some cases, these abductees are believed to be replaced by changelings, fairy substitutes that often bring misfortune or sickness to the family. These tales reflect the Aos Sí's complex and often capricious nature, highlighting the delicate balance required when dealing with these beings.

CULTURAL SIGNIFICANCE

The belief in the Aos Sí has played a significant role in shaping the cultural practices of Ireland. The fairies are deeply embedded in the rural traditions of the Irish people, influencing everything from agricultural practices to customs around childbirth and death. The reverence for the Aos Sí is evident in the numerous superstitions and rituals designed to protect against their displeasure, such as the careful maintenance of fairy forts or the avoidance of certain actions believed to provoke their wrath.

The Aos Sí are also a reflection of the Celtic worldview, where the natural and supernatural exist in a delicate balance, and the unseen forces of the world demand respect. They represent the idea that nature is alive with spirits and hidden powers, and that humanity must coexist carefully with these elements. In many ways, the Aos Sí personify the mystery and magic of the Irish landscape, embodying the cultural memory of a time when the world was filled with wonder and enchantment.

THE BANSHEE

The Banshee, known in Irish as Bean Sí or Bean Sidhe, meaning "woman of the mounds" or "fairy woman," is a supernatural figure often associated with death and the Otherworld.

This spectral being is believed to foretell the imminent death of a family member through her mournful wail, a sound that is said to chill the listener to the bone. The Banshee has become one of the most iconic figures in Irish folklore, reflecting both the fear and reverence for the supernatural that permeates Ireland's cultural traditions.

Appearance and Characteristics

The Banshee is typically depicted as a female spirit, and her appearance varies across different accounts. In some versions of the legend, she is described as a beautiful young woman with long, flowing hair, usually either silver, red, or dark. She often wears a cloak or flowing white garments, which add to her ethereal appearance. In other tales, she is portrayed as an old woman with withered skin, hollow eyes, and tattered clothes, her form reflecting the sorrow she bears. This dual representation symbolizes her connection with both beauty and decay, as well as the passage of life into death.

One of the defining features of the Banshee is her 'keening'—a mournful cry or wail that can be heard before the death of a loved one. This lament is piercing and filled with sorrow, and said to be so haunting that those who hear it are often overcome with dread. Her cry is a form of mourning, echoing the traditional Irish practice of keening over the dead, a role often performed by women known as "keeners." The Banshee's keening thus symbolizes a bridge between the mortal and spiritual realms, serving as a warning of what is to come.

ORIGINS AND MYTHOLOGICAL CONTEXT

The origins of the Banshee can be traced back to the ancient Tuatha Dé Danann, the mythical race of deities who once inhabited Ireland. It is believed that the Banshee was once a member of this divine race who, after their defeat and retreat into the Otherworld, became a harbinger of death. The mounds or sídhe that the Tuatha Dé Danann retreated into are closely linked with the Banshee, as she is said to dwell within these earthen hills. The Banshee, therefore, represents a deep connection to the ancestral spirits of Ireland, functioning as a spectral presence that traverses the boundary between life and death.

In Irish tradition, the Banshee is thought to be attached to specific families, particularly those with surnames beginning with "O'" or "Mac." Historically, her presence was often connected to noble families, but over time, her domain expanded to encompass all Irish families. This familial association further emphasizes her role as a guardian spirit—a figure who remains tied to her kin even beyond death, acting as a messenger of fate. The Banshee's lament is not intended as an act of malevolence but as a gesture of sorrow, mourning the loss of a loved one in her own spectral way.

ROLE AND SYMBOLISM

The Banshee's primary role is that of a death omen. Her presence is a harbinger of death, and those who hear her wail understand that a death in their family

is imminent. The symbolism of the Banshee is profound, reflecting the Celtic understanding of life and death as intertwined states of existence. Her appearance is not meant to cause harm; instead, she mourns the loss of a loved one, embodying the natural cycle of life and the inevitability of death. In this way, the Banshee is more of a tragic figure than a malevolent one—she grieves for the departed and warns the living of the coming sorrow.

The Banshee's keening can also be seen as a continuation of ancient Celtic mourning practices, where women played a key role in expressing collective grief. The act of keening was traditionally performed at funerals, an emotional lament that helped guide the deceased into the afterlife. The Banshee's supernatural keening, therefore, links her to this ritualistic expression of grief, highlighting her role as a spiritual guide who helps transition the soul from the mortal world to the Otherworld.

The presence of the Banshee also reflects the belief in an Otherworld, a place that coexists alongside the human world. This realm is populated by spirits and beings that influence the lives of mortals, often interacting with them in subtle and mysterious ways. The Banshee's connection to the Otherworld emphasizes the permeability of the boundary between life and death in Celtic mythology, a theme that is echoed in many Irish legends.

Above: "The Bunworth Banshee," by Thomas Crofton Croker, a woodcut illustration from *Fairy Legends and Traditions of the South of Ireland*, 1825; **Top**: "The Banshee Appeared," a metal-etched illustration from a publication of 1862; **Opposite:** Banshee, modern fantasy illustration, courtesy Jennifer Derrig/The Irish Jewelry Company

PÚCA | DULLAHAN | SELKIE

Above: A character dressed as a Púca during the 2019 Púca Festival in Athboy, County Meath, Ireland. The Festival was a celebration of the Celtic origin of the modern Halloween phenomenon; **Top:** An AI-generated modern fantasy interpretation of the Púca, by Flidia Foltchain, 2023 @ NightCafe Studio

THE PÚCA

The Púca (also spelled Pooka, Phooka, or Púka) is a shape-shifting creature known for its mischievous and unpredictable nature.

Considered one of the Aos Sí—the supernatural beings who inhabit the unseen world of Irish mythology—the Púca is a spirit of transformation, embodying both the playful and potentially dangerous aspects of the natural world. With the ability to take many different forms, this creature is known for its interactions with humans, which can range from benign tricks to terrifying pranks.

Appearance and Characteristics

As a shape-shifter, it commonly appears as a black horse with glowing eyes, a goat, or a large black dog, all of which emphasize its wild and mysterious character. Sometimes the Púca is depicted as a dark, human-like figure or even as a strange, almost demonic creature with animalistic features. In all its forms, the Púca is often described as having an eerie, otherworldly presence.

Its equine form is one of the most well-known representations, often involving stories where the Púca allows unsuspecting people to ride it. Once they are on its back, it races across the countryside, taking them on a frightening journey, only to throw them off at dawn in some remote location. Despite this potentially dangerous behavior, the Púca generally does not cause lasting harm, emphasizing its trickster-like nature rather than malevolence.

The Púca's behavior can vary widely. In some tales, it is a benevolent being, offering wise counsel or even assisting with farming tasks. In other stories, it is mischievous, stealing crops, frightening livestock, or leading travelers astray. This duality highlights the Púca's complex character—it is neither inherently good nor evil but embodies the unpredictability of the Otherworld and the untamed forces of nature.

THE DULLAHAN

The Dullahan is a spectral figure often depicted as a headless horseman riding a black steed. This terrifying being is considered a harbinger of death, known for its chilling appearance and sinister behavior.

The Dullahan carries its own head under one arm, with its face twisted into a grotesque grin and eyes that dart about, capable of seeing great distances even in the dark. The head itself is said to glow faintly, providing the Dullahan with light as it rides through the night.

The Dullahan's mount, a black horse with fiery eyes, gallops through the countryside, sometimes pulling a black carriage known as the Cóiste Bodhar—a "death coach" that signals the end for those who witness it. The Dullahan is known for calling out the name of the person whose death is imminent, at which point that individual is doomed to die. There is no way to prevent the Dullahan's approach; gates and locks mean nothing to it, as it can pass through barriers with ease. This fearsome figure is said to have an aversion to gold, which can be used

to ward it off temporarily. Though rarely described as malevolent toward those it doesn't pursue, its mere presence inspires fear and respect. The Dullahan serves as a grim reminder of mortality, symbolizing the inevitability of death and the supernatural forces that influence the human experience.

THE SELKIE

The Selkie is a mythical creature found in Irish and Scottish folklore, known for its ability to transform from a seal into a human. Selkies are said to live as seals in the sea but can shed their skins to take on human form on land. These transformations are often temporary, allowing them to walk as humans for a time, before they must return to the sea.

In human form, Selkies are described as beautiful, with an allure that often captures the attention of humans. Many tales involve a Selkie whose seal skin is stolen by a human, typically a fisherman, forcing the Selkie to remain in human form and marry the thief. Despite often forming loving families, the Selkie's longing for the sea never fades. In these stories, the Selkie eventually finds its stolen skin and returns to the ocean, leaving behind its human family, driven by an irresistible pull toward the water.

Selkies symbolize the tension between two worlds—the sea and the land—and the yearning for freedom. They embody themes of love, loss, and the powerful draw of the natural world. Their legends serve as a reminder of the mystery and allure of the ocean and the profound connection between humans and the sea that remains a significant element of Celtic folklore.

Above: The Selkie Statue in Mikladalur, on the Faroe Islands. Picture courtesy of Siegfried Rabanser, via Wikimedia Commons; **Main image, top left:** A gamer's depiction of the Dullahan, courtesy Reddit/Eldon Bling; **Top, right:** The "death coach" of the Dullahan, courtesy of *Kevin's Ireland*; **Center, right:** A more conventional 19th-century depiction of the Dullahan—"a spectral figure riding a black steed."

Above: The shape-shifting Kelpie, in its horse form, an AI-generated picture courtesy of NightCafe Studio; **Top, main image:** *Evening Calm, Study for The Kelpie*, Herbert James Draper, 1913, Oil on canvas. The Collection of the Lady Lever Art Gallery, Port Sunlight, Liverpool.

The Kelpie is a shape-shifting water spirit particularly associated with the rivers and lochs of Ireland and Scotland.

THE KELPIE

Often described as a horse, the Kelpie lures unsuspecting victims, typically children or travelers, to watery deaths.

In its horse form, the Kelpie appears as a magnificent, sleek, and strong animal, often standing by the water's edge. However, once mounted, the Kelpie's true nature is revealed as it plunges into the water, drowning its rider. The Kelpie's ability to transform is a key feature of its myth. It can appear as a beautiful horse or, in some stories, as a human, often a handsome man or a young woman, to deceive its victims. In human form, the Kelpie might use charm to lure people closer to the water's edge, before dragging them into the depths.

Although the Kelpie is primarily viewed as a malevolent creature, some tales hint at a more ambiguous nature, with a few Kelpies said to offer protection or act as guardians of waterways. Despite these variations, the Kelpie is most commonly feared for its connection to drowning and the treacherous nature of deep waters. In Scottish folklore, the Kelpie symbolizes the dangers of wild water and serves as a cautionary tale for those who might venture too close to dangerous rivers and lakes, reminding people of the untamable and sometimes deadly power of nature.

KELPIE | MERROW

The Merrow is a sea-dwelling creature similar to mermaids and mermen.

THE MERROW

The term is derived from the Irish word "muir" (sea) and "ógh" (maid), and these beings are often depicted as having the upper bodies of beautiful women or handsome men and the lower bodies of fish.

Female Merrows are typically portrayed as enchanting and benevolent, while male Merrows are less commonly described and are sometimes characterized as wilder and more dangerous.

Merrows are known for their connections to both the underwater world and the land. They are said to possess *cohuleen druith*, an enchanted cap or cloak, which allows them to move between the sea and the land. Without this cap, they are unable to return to their oceanic home, which has led to stories of humans taking a Merrow's cap in order to compel them to stay on land. Unlike other sea beings, Merrows are often friendly toward humans, sometimes even marrying them and raising families on land.

The Merrow represents a bridge between the mysterious underwater world and human life, embodying themes of love, freedom, and the allure of the unknown. The stories of Merrows often reflect the deep cultural relationship between the Irish people and the sea, capturing the beauty and the potential danger of the ocean while emphasizing the profound longing many feel for a different, freer life beyond the boundaries of their everyday world.

Above: A Merrow, pencil drawing, courtesy of *Ireland's Lore and Tales*, on Wordpress; **Below left**: Carved stone Merrow, Clonfert Cathedral, Clonfert, County Galway, Ireland; **Below right:** A Merrow coming to the aid of a drowning mariner. Courtesy of Ann Massey McElroy, Dark Emerald Tales & Travels.

LEPRECHAUNS

The Leprechaun is one of the most iconic figures in Irish mythology, known for its mischievous nature, association with hidden treasures, and distinct appearance.

Above left: An Arthur Rackham interpretation of the "little fellahs" from a strange book published in 1916, at the height of the Battle of the Somme, called *The Allies' Fairy Book*, which included illustrated folklore tales from Russia, Great Britain, and France; **Above right:** "Little Folk Leprechauns," from 1873, complete with drunken Irish stereotype

These small, magical beings are considered part of the Aos Sí, a supernatural race akin to fairies or elves. Leprechauns occupy a special place in Irish folklore, often symbolizing the untamed, playful, and trickster elements of the Celtic spirit.

Origins and Description

The origins of the Leprechaun can be traced back to early Celtic mythology. They are believed to be a type of solitary fairy, distinct from the more social fairies or other members of the Aos Sí. The name "Leprechaun" is thought to come from the Irish term *leipreachán*, which may derive from *luchorpán* meaning "small body." This etymology highlights their diminutive size, which is a defining feature of these beings. Leprechauns are typically portrayed as small, elderly men dressed in old-fashioned clothing—often wearing a green coat, buckled shoes, and a hat. Originally,

Leprechauns were depicted wearing red, but over time, green became more closely associated with them, reflecting the national color of Ireland. They are also frequently shown with a leather apron, emphasizing their role as shoemakers.

Personality and Characteristics

Leprechauns are known for their trickster nature. They are clever, resourceful, and often quite mischievous, delighting in playing pranks on humans. Despite this playful streak, they are also portrayed as somewhat solitary and aloof, often preferring their own company to that of other fairies or humans. The stories emphasize that Leprechauns are not malevolent but can be sly and crafty, always looking for opportunities to outwit those who try to catch them.

One of the most well-known aspects of Leprechaun folklore is their connection to hidden treasure, often said to be a pot of gold hidden at the end of a rainbow. According to legend, if a human catches a Leprechaun, they may be able to demand that he reveal the location of his treasure. However, outwitting a Leprechaun is no easy task; they are adept at trickery and will do anything to escape, often employing clever tactics to distract or deceive their captors.

Leprechauns are often described as cobblers or shoemakers. The sound of the Leprechaun's hammering is often said to be one of the few clues that can lead to his discovery. If one is fortunate enough to follow the sound and catch the Leprechaun, it may lead to an encounter filled with both risk and potential reward. However, Leprechauns are notoriously evasive, and those seeking their gold are usually left empty-handed, either due to their own greed or because they fall prey to the Leprechaun's cunning tricks.

Top left: *Leprechauns and Fairies*. A French 19th-century illustration; **Top right** and **above**: Modern fantasy AI illustrations of Leprechauns. It seems that Leprechauns are now typecast to always be depicted with ginger beards and Emerald Isle Green top hats and waistcoats...

CHANGELINGS

A Changeling is a creature found in Irish folklore, as well as broader Celtic and European folklore, often regarded as a fairy child that has been left in place of a human infant.

Above: A mid-19th-century book illustration with the caption: "Jennet Francis struggles with fairies who are stealing her daughter..."; **Top left:** A typical 1930s children's illustration of fairies gazing enviously in a newborn's crib; **Top right:** *The Changeling*, by Henry Fuseli, the 18th-century Swiss artist who lived and worked in England

The phenomenon is believed to occur when the Aos Sí (fairies or "the people of the mounds") or other supernatural beings become envious of a human child and decide to take it, leaving behind their own offspring.

Characteristics of a Changeling

Changelings are typically described as having unusual characteristics that differentiate them from human children. They may appear sickly or have a strange demeanor, fail to grow properly, or exhibit odd behaviors. In some cases, they are said to be much more demanding, constantly crying or showing insatiable hunger, and lacking the normal traits of human infants. Despite being the size of a baby, a changeling may possess the features of an elderly person, reinforcing their otherworldly origins.

Changelings were also believed to possess unusual abilities or talents beyond what a human child could demonstrate. They might speak fluently at an early age or display an unsettling level of intelligence. Often, their true identity could be detected by their uncanny behavior, such as an aversion to Christian symbols, inability to look people in the eye, or mysterious laughter. These peculiar traits were taken as signs that a child was not entirely human and had been replaced by a being from the Otherworld.

THE CELTIC WORLD
Celtic Changeling Folklore in Europe

Variations on the Celtic changeling myth can be found in a number of European traditions. While the concept remains the same, each culture has a unique take on the myth. In German folklore, changelings are known as *Wechselbälg* or *Wechselkind,* and they are thought to be left by elves or dwarves. German legends often suggest that fairies are drawn to particularly healthy or attractive human children. Many believed that making the changeling laugh would reveal their true form. In Scandinavian folklore, trolls are believed to leave their own offspring, known as *bortbytingar* in Swedish, in place of the human child. The changeling left behind is usually sickly or unusual in appearance. In Poland, the changeling is called an *odmieniec,* a sickly child left by demons or otherworldly beings. Slavic folklore sometimes describes changelings as having a voracious appetite, depleting a household's resources, and other unusual physical and behavioral traits.

Origins and Reasons for Substitution

The belief in changelings is deeply rooted in Celtic mythology, particularly in the idea of the Otherworld—a parallel realm inhabited by supernatural beings. The Aos Sí were known to interact with the human world, often out of jealousy or a desire for something they lacked in their realm. There were several reasons given for why fairies might take a human child and leave a changeling in its place. One belief was that fairies were drawn to the beauty of human children or their vitality, seeking to improve their own offspring through contact with human society.

Protective Measures and Folklore Practices

The fear of having one's child taken by fairies led to various protective practices. Parents would take numerous precautions to ensure that their children were safe from being swapped with a changeling. Iron, particularly in the form of scissors or a nail, was often placed near a baby's crib, as iron was believed to repel fairies. Other methods included keeping a lit candle near the baby or ensuring that the infant was baptized as soon as possible, as Christian rites were thought to provide protection from the Otherworld's influence.

In some stories, it was said that the only way to reveal a changeling's true nature was through trickery or extreme actions that would force the fairy to reveal itself. For example, the parent might pretend to cook the changeling in an empty eggshell, which would make the fairy laugh and reveal its knowledge far beyond that of a child. Once exposed, the changeling would often flee or be reclaimed by its fairy kin, with the human child sometimes being returned in exchange.

However, these practices also reflected a darker side of folklore, as some parents, out of desperation, resorted to harsh or harmful measures to "test" a suspected changeling. This fear and the resulting actions demonstrate the very real anxieties people had about the well-being of their children in a world where infant mortality was high, and many illnesses were poorly understood.

Above: The devil steals a baby and leaves a changeling behind, detail from *The Legend of St. Stephen* by Martino di Bartolomeo, circa early 1400s; **Inset, top:** *The Princess and the Trolls* by Swedish artist John Bauer, 1913

THE FOMORIANS

The Fomorians are supernatural beings, often depicted as chaotic and monstrous, symbolizing the primal, untamed aspects of nature, in opposition to the more cultured and orderly Tuatha Dé Danann.

Above: A traditional interpretation of Balor of the Evil Eye, king of the Fomorians, sourced from Mythlok; **Top:** Modern fantasy interpretations of the supernatural race of the Fomorians, sourced from Irish History

They are believed to have been among the first inhabitants of Ireland, representing the destructive forces of nature, including the sea, darkness, and chaos.

Descriptions of the Fomorians vary, with some portraying them as grotesque and deformed giants, while others are said to be beautiful but dangerous. They are often depicted with misshapen bodies, sometimes possessing a single eye, arm, or leg.

The Fomorians were known as adversaries of the Tuatha Dé Danann, the gods of Irish myth. They ruled Ireland until the arrival of the Tuatha Dé Danann, leading to a series of battles for control.

One of the most famous tales involving the Fomorians is the Second Battle of Moytura, *Mag Tuired*, where the Fomorian king Balor of the Evil Eye was killed by his grandson Lugh, a hero of the Tuatha Dé Danann.

The Fomorians symbolize the primal, untamed aspects of nature, in opposition to the more cultured and orderly Tuatha Dé Danann.

The stories of the Fomorians reveal their role as both adversaries and, in some instances, as part of the lineage of Irish gods and heroes, underscoring their complex relationship with the later mythic races of Ireland.

Left: "Ambassadors of the Fir Bolg and Tuath Dé meet before the Battle of Moytura." An illustration by Stephen Reid from *Myths & Legends of the Celtic Race*, by Thomas Rolleston, 1911 (see pages 72–73); **Below:** "The arrival of the Milesians," also by Stephen Reid, and also from *Myths & Legends of the Celtic Race*, by Thomas Rolleston, 1911.

THE FIR BOLG

The Fir Bolg are a race of people in Irish mythology, said to be one of several early tribes to settle in Ireland before the arrival of the Tuatha Dé Danann.

According to legend, they were descendants of the Nemedians, an earlier group who had fled Ireland after being oppressed by the Fomorians. The Fir Bolg eventually returned to Ireland after years of enslavement and wandering, settling the land and dividing it into provinces.

The Fir Bolg were known as a practical and hardworking people, and they are credited with bringing structure and agricultural development to Ireland.

When the Tuatha Dé Danann arrived, they demanded part of the land from the Fir Bolg, which ultimately led to the First Battle of Moytura. Despite their courage and determination, the Fir Bolg were defeated by the Tuatha Dé Danann, though their bravery in battle was honored by their opponents.

The Fir Bolg are remembered for their contribution to the early mythical history of Ireland and their tenacity in defending their homeland. Though ultimately defeated, their legacy persisted in Irish mythology as part of the complex tapestry of the mythical peoples who inhabited Ireland before the arrival of the Milesians, who were considered the ancestors of the modern Irish.

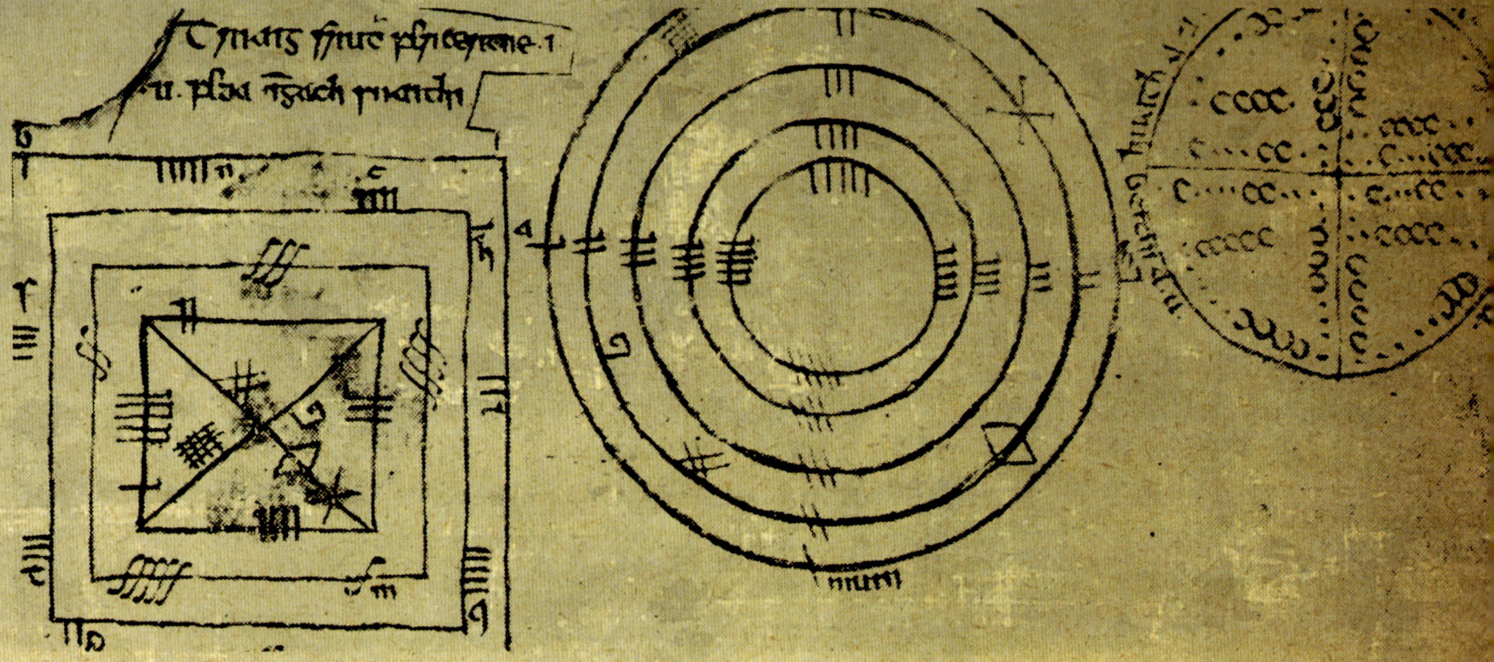

THE MYTHOLOGICAL CYCLE

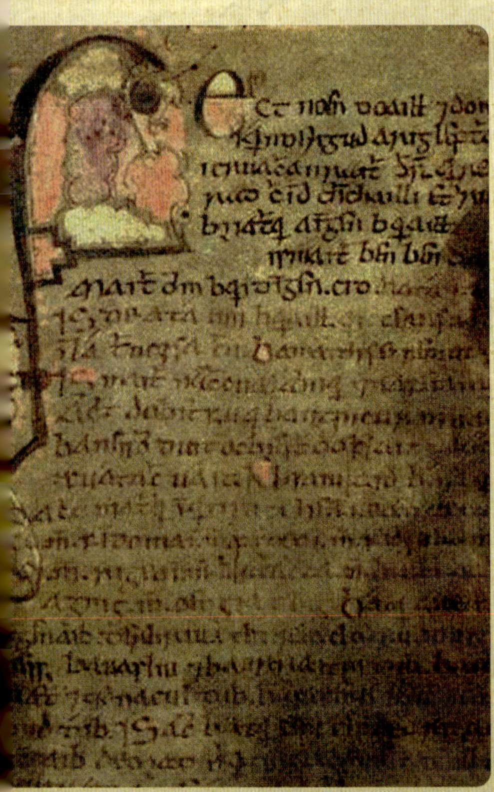

The Mythological Cycle is one of the four major cycles of Irish mythology, alongside the Ulster Cycle, the Fenian Cycle, and the Historical Cycle. It is the oldest of the cycles and centers on the gods, early supernatural races, and the mythical origins of Ireland.

The Mythological Cycle tells the story of a series of invasions by different groups, culminating in the arrival of the Milesians, who are considered the ancestors of the Irish people. These stories are an essential part of the mythological heritage of Ireland, blending folklore, history, and religious belief into a narrative that explains the origins of the land and its people.

SOURCES AND MANUSCRIPTS

The Mythological Cycle is preserved in several medieval manuscripts, including the *Book of Invasions* (*Lebor Gabála Érenn*), which offers an account of how Ireland was settled by successive waves of invaders. Other significant sources include the *Book of Leinster* and the *Book of Ballymote*. These manuscripts, compiled by Christian monks, drew from much older oral traditions, blending myth, pseudo-history, and biblical influences. Although the content of these texts was shaped by their Christian scribes, the core of the Mythological Cycle remains a reflection of Ireland's pre-Christian worldview.

INVASIONS AND KEY GROUPS

The Mythological Cycle is largely focused on the mythic history of Ireland through a series of invasions by different supernatural groups, each of which brought its own unique influence to the land. The first inhabitants were Cessair and her people, who came to Ireland before the Biblical Flood, followed by the

Partholonians, who settled the land only to be wiped out by a plague. After them came the Nemedians, who struggled against the Fomorians—a race of monstrous beings representing chaos and the untamed forces of nature.

The Fir Bolg were the next group to arrive, establishing a structured society before being challenged by the Tuatha Dé Danann, a group of god-like beings and one of the most prominent and revered races in Irish mythology.

The Tuatha Dé Danann brought with them advanced knowledge of magic and craftsmanship, representing a golden age of prosperity and connection with the Otherworld. They fought two significant battles at Mag Tuired: the first against the Fir Bolg, and the second against the Fomorians. Their eventual defeat by the Milesians marked the end of their dominion, after which they retreated into the mounds and became the Aos Sí, or fairy people.

THEMES AND SYMBOLISM

The Mythological Cycle presents themes of conflict, settlement, and transformation, depicting the struggle for control of Ireland between successive waves of supernatural beings. The series of invasions serves not only as a mythic history but also as a symbolic explanation for the land's spiritual power and its connection to the Otherworld. The Tuatha Dé Danann, in particular, are portrayed as embodiments of divine qualities, representing the forces of creativity, wisdom, and the magical aspects of the natural world.

The conflicts with the Fomorians, often depicted as dark and chaotic beings, also reflect a recurring theme of balance between creation and destruction. These stories illustrate the duality between the life-giving elements of culture and civilization and the primal, often destructive, forces of nature. The Second Battle of Mag Tuired, in which Lugh defeats his grandfather Balor, epitomizes this struggle, symbolizing the triumph of light and order over darkness and chaos.

Above: Nuada, the first king of the Tuatha Dé Danann, modern fantasy image sourced from Old World Gods; **Opposite, top:** Fragments from *The Book of Ballymote* (*Leabhar Bhaile an Mhóta*), written in 1390 AD, near Ballymote, now in County Sligo, but then in the tuath of Corann. **Opposite, bottom:** Vellum manuscript page from the *Book of Leinster*, Folio 53. *The Book of Leinster*, (*Lebor Laignech*), is a medieval Irish manuscript compiled by Christian monks, circa 1160 AD. Courtesy of Trinity College Dublin.

NOTABLE FIGURES

The Mythological Cycle of Irish mythology is populated by numerous notable figures, primarily drawn from the Tuatha Dé Danann, the legendary beings who ruled Ireland before the arrival of the Milesians.

Above: "Nuada of the Silver Hand"; **Top left:** Modern fantasy digitally-generated image of Brigid, the Irish goddess of healing and poetry, from Old World Gods; **Top right:** Another fantasy illustration of Lugh, courtesy of Paganista

These figures are central to the myths that explore the origins of Ireland, its divine heritage, and the interplay between supernatural forces. Key individuals like Dagda, Morrigan, Lugh, Nuada, and Brigid each play vital roles in the tales that form the Mythological Cycle, contributing to the narrative of battles, magic, and the shaping of Ireland's mystical landscape.

LUGH

Lugh is one of the most celebrated heroes of the Mythological Cycle, renowned for his skills and versatility.

Known as Lugh Lámhfhada (Lugh of the Long Arm), he is a god associated with light, craftsmanship, and skill in many disciplines. He arrives at the court of the Tuatha Dé Danann at a crucial moment, offering his talents and ultimately leading them in the Second Battle of Moytura. During this battle, Lugh famously defeats his grandfather Balor, the fearsome one-eyed king of the Fomorians, thus securing victory for the Tuatha Dé Danann.

NUADA

Nuada Airgetlám (Nuada of the Silver Hand) was the first king of the Tuatha Dé Danann and a respected leader.

He lost his arm in the First Battle of Moytura against the Fir Bolg, which

initially made him unfit to rule, as kings were required to be physically whole. A silver arm was crafted for him by the physician Dian Cecht, earning him the name "Nuada of the Silver Hand." Nuada was later able to reclaim the throne, only to lose it again when Bres, a half-Fomorian, temporarily took power.

BRIGID

Brigid is a multifaceted figure in the Mythological Cycle, revered as a goddess of healing, poetry, and smithcraft.

She is one of the daughters of the Dagda and holds a prominent position among the Tuatha Dé Danann. Brigid is associated with fire and inspiration, and she is also connected to fertility and the protection of homes and livestock. Her influence extends beyond mythology into the cultural practices of Ireland, where she became one of the most significant deities, eventually merging with the Christian figure of Saint Brigid.

BALOR

Balor of the Evil Eye is a fearsome leader of the Fomorians, representing the forces of chaos and destruction. He is known for his one giant, poisonous eye, which could kill anyone upon whom its gaze fell.

During the Second Battle of Mag Tuired, Balor played a pivotal role against the Tuatha Dé Danann until he was slain by his grandson Lugh, fulfilling a prophecy that he would die at the hands of his own kin. Balor's defeat marked a turning point in the struggle between the Tuatha Dé Danann and the Fomorians.

Above: Balor of the Evil Eye, the leader of the Fomorians; **Top:** Another impression of Nuada, the first king of the Tuatha Dé Danann—"Nuada of the Silver Hand." Courtesy of Old World Gods

THE BATTLES OF MOYTURA

The story of the Battles of Moytura, or *Mag Tuired*, tells of two legendary conflicts fought between the supernatural races of Ireland during the time of the Mythological Cycle. These battles were crucial in determining the fate of the land, involving the Tuatha Dé Danann, the divine beings of Ireland, and their adversaries, the Fir Bolg, and the Fomorians.

The First Battle of Moytura began when the Tuatha Dé Danann arrived in Ireland. They were a powerful race of deities, skilled in magic and craftsmanship, having traveled from far lands. At that time, Ireland was ruled by the Fir Bolg, a people who had long controlled the island. Seeking peace, the Tuatha Dé Danann asked for a portion of land to settle, but the Fir Bolg refused. Conflict was inevitable.

The two sides met on the plains of Moytura, and the battle was fierce. The Fir Bolg fought valiantly to defend their dominion, but the Tuatha Dé Danann's superior magic and strength gradually turned the tide. Among the Tuatha Dé Danann was their king, Nuada, a skilled warrior who led his people into battle. During the fighting, Nuada faced the Fir Bolg champion, Sreng. In a vicious exchange, Sreng struck Nuada's arm from his body. Although the Tuatha Dé Danann ultimately emerged victorious, the loss of Nuada's arm was significant, as it rendered him physically unfit to rule according to the customs of his people. The Fir Bolg were not destroyed but allowed to retain a portion of Ireland, acknowledging the Tuatha Dé Danann's dominance.

After the battle, Nuada's severed arm was replaced with a silver prosthetic by the skilled healer Dian Cecht, and he became known as Nuada of the Silver Hand. However, because he was no longer whole, leadership temporarily passed to Bres, a half-Fomorian who would go on to rule with cruelty, favoring his Fomorian kin over the Tuatha Dé Danann. Bres's tyranny created unrest, and the Tuatha Dé Danann eventually sought to overthrow him, leading to the Second Battle of Moytura.

The Second Battle of Moytura was fought between the Tuatha Dé Danann and the

Fomorians, a race of monstrous beings associated with chaos and destruction. Under Bres's rule, the Tuatha Dé Danann were subjected to heavy tribute and oppression by the Fomorians, led by their fearsome king, Balor of the Evil Eye. Balor's gaze was deadly, capable of killing anyone upon whom it fell. However, a prophecy foretold that Balor would be killed by his own grandson.

Lugh, a young hero of the Tuatha Dé Danann, rose to challenge Balor's reign. Lugh was skilled in all arts and crafts, earning him a place among the gods, and his arrival signaled a turning point for the Tuatha Dé Danann. In preparation for the battle, the gods rallied their forces, while Balor brought forth his formidable army of Fomorians. The clash was fierce and desperate, with magic and weaponry colliding on the battlefield.

During the battle, Lugh confronted his grandfather, Balor. As Balor prepared to unleash his deadly gaze, Lugh hurled his magic spear that struck Balor in his eye, killing him and fulfilling the prophecy. With Balor's death, the Fomorians were defeated, and the Tuatha Dé Danann regained control of Ireland, ending Bres's rule.

Right: Lugh charges into battle with his magical spear. According to Irish mythology, the Spear of Lugh is one of Ireland's seven treasures. Forged by the god Lugh to use against Balor of the Evil Eye, legend said that whoever held it would be victorious, and that it was so hot to touch it had to be kept with the blade in cold water. The spear, once thrown, always came back to Lugh—after always hitting its mark. Illustration by H. R. Millar, 1905; **Opposite:** "Ambassadors of the Fir Bolg and Tuath Dé meet before the Battle of Moytura." An illustration by Stephen Reid from *Myths & Legends of the Celtic Race*, by Thomas Rolleston, 1911.

THE CHILDREN OF LIR

There once lived a nobleman named Lir, who was married to a kind and beautiful woman, Aobh. Together, they had four children: a daughter, Fionnuala, and three sons, Aodh, and the twins, Fiachra and Conn.

Lir loved his children dearly, and they were known throughout the land for their beauty and grace. Sadly, Aobh died shortly after the birth of the twins, leaving Lir and the children heartbroken.

To ease his sorrow and care for his children, Lir married Aobh's sister, Aoife. At first, Aoife was kind and loving toward the children, but as time passed, jealousy grew in her heart. She resented the love and attention that Lir lavished upon his children and began to feel neglected. Unable to bear it any longer, Aoife devised a terrible plan to rid herself of the children.

One day, Aoife took the children on a journey to visit their grandfather, Bodb Derg, the king of the Tuatha Dé Danann. On the way, they stopped at Lake Derravaragh. There, consumed by her jealousy, Aoife used her magic to transform the children into four beautiful white swans. Her spell condemned them to live in this form for 900 years: 300 years on Lake Derravaragh, 300 years on the Sea of Moyle, and 300 years on the waters of Inis Gluaire. They would only be freed when they heard the bell of a Christian church.

After casting the spell, Aoife was overcome with guilt and regret. Though she could not reverse the curse, she granted the children the ability to speak and sing beautifully in their swan forms. She then disappeared, leaving the enchanted children behind.

When Lir discovered what had happened to his beloved children, he was devastated. He searched the lake and found the four swans, who called out to him with human voices, telling him of Aoife's betrayal. Though he could not break the curse, Lir visited the swans often at Lake Derravaragh, and their beautiful singing brought peace to his heart.

After 300 years, the time came for the children to leave Lake Derravaragh and move to the Sea of Moyle. The waters of Moyle were harsh and stormy, and the swans endured great suffering during this period. Though they stayed together, they faced bitter cold, hunger, and loneliness. Still, they found comfort in each other's company and waited patiently for the day they could be free.

After another 300 years, the swans moved to their final destination at Inis Gluaire. By now, Ireland had changed greatly, and Christianity had spread across the land. One day, the sound of a distant bell reached their ears. Knowing that their time as swans was nearly over, they made their way to the shore.

There, they met a Christian monk named Caomhog, who baptized them and broke the spell. However, as the swans transformed back into their human forms, the years they had spent as swans caught up to them. They became old and frail, soon passing away. Caomhog buried them together, so they would never be separated again.

Above: *The Children of Lir*, by John Duncan, 1924. Tempera on canvas, tondo. Dundee Art Galleries and Museums Collection

THE WOOING OF ÉTAÍN

Once there was a beautiful woman named Étaín, born of the Tuatha Dé Danann, whose radiance was unmatched. Her beauty captivated all who saw her, and tales of her grace and charm spread throughout the land.

High King Eochaid Airem, ruler of Ireland, had heard of her beauty and desired her as his queen. He was determined to win her, but the story of Étaín's life and love was far more complex than he realized, for Étaín had been part of a tragic and ancient love story.

Long before Étaín's time among the mortals, she had been loved by Midir, one of the lords of the Tuatha Dé Danann. Midir lived in the Otherworld, the magical realm of the gods. His wife, Fuamnach, was powerful and skilled in magic, but when Midir's love for Étaín blossomed, Fuamnach's jealousy grew fierce. Enraged by Midir's affection for Étaín, Fuamnach cast a cruel spell upon her, turning Étaín into a pool of water. From the water, Étaín was transformed again into a butterfly, cursed to drift through the winds, never to return to her beloved Midir.

As a butterfly, Étaín was constantly blown by the winds, suffering for many long years. She was buffeted by storms and left helpless by Fuamnach's magic. However, Midir, still devoted to her, found her and cared for her in secret, feeding her nectar and protecting her as best he could. Despite his efforts, Fuamnach's wrath knew no bounds, and she unleashed a tempest that tore Étaín away from Midir. Blown far from him, Étaín drifted for seven years until she eventually came to rest on the roof of a house belonging to the wife of an Ulster chieftain.

In this household, Étaín was accidentally swallowed by the woman, who became pregnant with her. Étaín was reborn into the mortal world, unaware of her former life as a goddess. Her beauty remained, and as she grew, her radiance became even more enchanting. She was raised as the daughter of the Ulster chieftain and was known far and wide for her charm. This is where High King Eochaid Airem first heard of her. He sought her out and asked for her hand in marriage. Étaín, unaware of her divine origins or her past love for Midir, accepted, and the two were wed.

Étaín became Eochaid's queen, and they were happy together. However, her past was not forgotten, for Midir had never given up his love for her. After many years, Midir decided to reclaim his beloved. He traveled from the Otherworld to the court of Eochaid in disguise, intent on winning Étaín back. However, he could not simply take her by force, for Eochaid was a powerful king. Instead, Midir hatched a clever plan.

One day, Midir approached Eochaid's court in the guise of a stranger and challenged the king to a game of fidchell, a strategic board game. Eochaid, being a proud and skilled player, accepted the challenge. The stakes were high, with Eochaid wagering his wealth and possessions. But Midir was no ordinary player, and he began to win, one game after another. Eochaid lost cattle, horses, and treasures, yet his pride compelled him to continue. Finally, Midir asked for one last wager: a single kiss from Étaín if he won. Desperate to win back his losses, Eochaid agreed.

Midir won the game, and when he came to collect his prize, he revealed his true identity and asked for not just a kiss but for Étaín to leave with him. Shocked, Eochaid refused to give up his queen. But Midir, determined to reclaim his lost love, promised to return in one month to take Étaín away.

As the month passed, Eochaid prepared his fortress, ordering his men to guard every door and window, hoping to prevent Midir from taking Étaín. The night Midir promised to return arrived, and Eochaid sat surrounded by his warriors, his queen by his side. Midir appeared before them, this time in his true form, as a god of the Tuatha Dé Danann, his otherworldly power radiating from him. He asked once more for Étaín, and Eochaid refused. But Midir was undeterred.

In an instant, Midir swept Étaín into his arms, and the two rose into the air, transforming into swans. Together, they flew out of the fortress through the smoke hole in the roof, soaring into the night sky. Eochaid, furious, sent his men after them, but it was in vain. Midir had taken Étaín back to the Otherworld.

Heartbroken and determined to reclaim his wife, Eochaid sought the help of druids and wise men. They advised him to find the sídhe, the entrances to the Otherworld, where Midir might have taken Étaín. Eochaid ordered his men to dig up every hill in Ireland, searching for the entrance to Midir's kingdom. His search eventually led him to Midir's fortress.

Midir, seeing that Eochaid would not relent, appeared before him and offered him a final challenge. He presented Eochaid with fifty identical women, all of whom appeared to be Étaín. Midir told Eochaid that if he could identify his true wife among the women, he could have her back. Eochaid studied each woman carefully, but they all looked the same. After much deliberation, he chose one, believing her to be Étaín.

For a time, Eochaid believed he had won back his queen. The woman bore him a daughter, but later, the truth was revealed: the woman was not Étaín at all, but her daughter from her previous life with Midir. The real Étaín remained in the Otherworld with her true love, Midir. Eochaid, realizing the depth of the love between Étaín and Midir, was left to accept his fate. He had unknowingly taken Étaín's daughter as his wife, while the real Étaín lived on in the Otherworld, reunited with the love she had been separated from for so long.

Above: "Midir took Étaín into his arms, and they rose into the air." Illustration by Stephen Reid, from *The High Deeds of Finn*, by Thomas Rolleston, 1910

THE DREAM OF AENGUS

Aengus, the god of love and youth, lived in the Brú na Bóinne, a grand and magical palace along the River Boyne.

One night, as he slept, Aengus had a vivid dream of a beautiful woman. She was unlike anyone he had ever seen—tall, graceful, and radiating a light that captivated his soul. She sang a hauntingly sweet melody, and Aengus was filled with an intense longing for her. When he awoke, the image of the woman lingered in his mind, and he found himself yearning for her presence.

Night after night, the same dream returned. Each time, the woman appeared more beautiful and more alluring. She would stand at a distance, singing her enchanting song, but always out of reach. Aengus's heart was consumed by his desire for her, and he became restless. He could neither eat nor sleep without thinking of her, and soon he became pale and weak from the longing that had overtaken him.

Distressed by his condition, Aengus sought the help of his mother, Boann, the river goddess. He told her of the woman who appeared in his dreams, and Boann, seeing her son's torment, promised to help. She searched far and wide for the woman who matched Aengus's description, but her efforts were in vain. At last, Boann turned to Aengus's father, the Dagda, one of the most powerful gods in the Tuatha Dé Danann, for assistance. The Dagda sent messengers across Ireland to find the mysterious woman. After a year of searching, they returned with news: the woman Aengus had dreamed of was Caer Ibormeith, the daughter of Ethal Anbuail, a prince of the Sidhe. Caer lived in Connacht, but there was a problem.

Caer was not an ordinary woman; she had the ability to transform into a swan. Every year, on the festival of Samhain, she would transform into a swan and remain in this form for half of the year.

Upon hearing this, Aengus set out to find Caer. He traveled to Connacht and approached her father, Ethal Anbuail, who reluctantly revealed that his daughter could be found on the lake of the Dragon's Mouth, along with 150 other maidens, all of whom would transform into swans on Samhain. Aengus was told that if he could identify her in her swan form, he could marry her.

When the day of Samhain arrived, Aengus went to the lake and watched as the maidens transformed into swans. With a heart full of hope, he called out to Caer, and she responded, recognizing him from his dreams. She agreed to go with him if he, too, could take the form of a swan. Aengus transformed into a swan, and together they flew across the lake, singing the same beautiful song Aengus had heard in his dreams.

Their song was so sweet that it put all who heard it into a deep sleep for three days and nights. Aengus and Caer flew back to Brú na Bóinne, where they lived together in joy and harmony for the rest of their days.

Left: *The Dream of Aengus*. Caer comes to Aengus with her hauntingly sweet melody, in his vivid, recurring dream. Chromolithograph from a painting by E. Wallcousins, from *Celtic Myth and Legend* by Charles Squire, London 1900.

The Ulster Cycle focuses on the heroic deeds, battles, and tragic fates of the warriors of Ulster, particularly during the reign of the legendary king Conchobar mac Nessa.

The tales of the Ulster Cycle are set in a heroic age, where honor, loyalty, and rivalry play central roles in the lives of warriors and kings. The cycle is rich with themes of personal glory, fate, and the tension between the individual hero and societal obligations.

The stories take place mostly in the northern province of Ulster, revolving around the warriors of the Red Branch, an elite group of fighters serving under King Conchobar. One of the most prominent figures in the Ulster Cycle is the young hero Cú Chulainn, whose extraordinary feats of strength and courage dominate many of the tales. He is a semi-divine figure, the son of the god Lugh and the mortal woman Deichtine, and his adventures are central to the cycle's exploration of heroism and sacrifice.

THE ULSTER CYCLE

The Ulster Cycle is the second of the four major cycles of Irish mythology, alongside the Mythological Cycle, the Fenian Cycle, and the Historical Cycle.

A key element of the Ulster Cycle is the tension between Ulster and its rival provinces, particularly Connacht, ruled by Queen Medb and her consort, Ailill. The most famous story of the cycle, the *Táin Bó Cúailnge* (The Cattle Raid of Cooley), depicts a massive conflict between Ulster and Connacht, sparked by Medb's desire to possess a prized bull. Cú Chulainn, who defends Ulster single-handedly while the rest of the warriors are incapacitated by a curse, is the central figure of the tale, exemplifying the heroic ideals of strength, bravery, and loyalty.

The Ulster Cycle also delves into the personal relationships and tragic destinies of its characters. The love stories of Deirdre and Naoise, or Cú Chulainn and Emer, often end in sorrow, reflecting the harsh realities of the warrior's life. Personal honor and vengeance often lead to cycles of violence and retribution, highlighting the fragility of peace and the inevitability of conflict in a warrior society.

Unlike the Mythological Cycle, which is populated by gods and supernatural beings, the Ulster Cycle features largely human characters with semi-divine or heroic qualities. The gods still play a role in influencing the events, but the focus is on human action, decision-making, and the consequences of those choices. The cycle also presents a society deeply rooted in a warrior ethos, where personal reputation, loyalty to one's lord, and success in battle are the measures of a person's worth.

The Ulster Cycle offers a glimpse into the heroic age of Ireland, blending historical elements with myth and legend. It reflects the complex relationships between kings, warriors, and rivals, and its stories have endured for many hundreds of years, capturing the imagination with their tales of bravery, loyalty, and the often tragic costs of heroism.

Opposite: *Cuchulainn*, a pencil sketch by John Duncan, the Scottish folklorist painter, circa early 20th-century. Courtesy National Galleries of Scotland

CÚ CHULAINN

Cú Chulainn is the most famous hero of the Ulster Cycle. Known as the "Hound of Ulster," he is a demigod, the son of the god Lugh and the mortal woman Deichtine.

Cú Chulainn is renowned for his extraordinary combat skills, bravery, and single-handed defense of Ulster during the famous conflict known as the Cattle Raid of Cooley. He is characterized by his ability to enter a battle frenzy, or *ríastrad*, in which he transforms into an unstoppable force. Despite his strength, Cú Chulainn's story is marked by tragedy, as he is fated to die young and meet a heroic yet sorrowful end.

CONCHOBAR MAC NESSA

Conchobar mac Nessa is the king of Ulster and a central figure in many of the Ulster Cycle's tales.

He is portrayed as a wise and powerful leader, though his decisions sometimes lead to tragic consequences. Conchobar's rise to power began under unusual circumstances—his mother, Ness, engineered his kingship by striking a deal with Ulster's rulers, making him king for a short term which, by turns, eventually became permanent.

Conchobar's reign is fraught with conflict, including the tension between Ulster and the neighboring kingdom of Connacht.

QUEEN MEDB

Queen Medb, the formidable ruler of Connacht, is one of the most intriguing figures of the Ulster Cycle.

Medb is a powerful and ambitious queen, known for her role in leading the forces of Connacht in the Cattle Raid of Cooley. She is portrayed as a strong and independent leader, but also as manipulative and ruthless. Her desire to claim the Brown Bull of Cooley leads to the conflict between Connacht and Ulster, with Cú Chulainn serving as Ulster's primary defender. Medb's relationship with her

NOTABLE FIGURES

husband, Ailill, and her former lover, Fergus mac Róich, adds complexity to her character.

FERGUS MAC RÓICH

Fergus mac Róich is a former king of Ulster who plays a prominent role in the Ulster Cycle.

After being betrayed by Conchobar, Fergus goes into exile and joins Queen Medb in Connacht. He is depicted as a loyal and honorable warrior, but his divided loyalties create tension. Fergus serves as a father figure to Cú Chulainn and holds deep respect for the young hero. Despite his conflicts with Conchobar, Fergus remains a key figure in the Cattle Raid of Cooley, fighting on the side of Connacht while still holding on to his past in Ulster.

OTHER NOTABLE FIGURES

Other notable figures include Deirdre, whose tragic love story with Naoise leads to her death and the exile of Fergus, and Scáthach, the legendary warrior woman who trains Cú Chulainn in combat. The cycle also features figures like Bricriu, whose mischief often stirs up conflict among the heroes, and Eochaid, who plays a role in the larger political landscape.

Right: A grief-stricken Cuchulain carries his dead foster-brother Ferdiad across the river. Chromolithograph from an illustration by Stephen Reid, from Eleanor Hull's *Cuchulain: The Hound of Ulster*, Harrap, London, 1909; **Opposite:** Fergus mac Róich, depicted in earlier, happy times, carrying Sétanta—who was to become Cú Chulainn, "the Hound of Culain"—on his shoulder. Illustrated by George Denham, 1909, and from the *Irish Fairy Book*, edited by Alfred Perceval Graves, 1917.

THE BIRTH OF CÚ CHULAINN

One day, Deichtine, the sister of Conchobar mac Nessa, King of Ulster, was helping to care for the King's horses with a group of companions...

As they worked, a strange thing happened—a flock of birds appeared, descended upon the field, and began to eat the newly-sown crop. Determined to drive the birds away, Deichtine and her companions followed the flock, which led them far from home. Eventually, they lost track of the birds and, as night fell, they sought shelter in a nearby house.

The house they found was not ordinary. A man and his wife welcomed them warmly, offering them food and rest. That night, the wife of the man gave birth to a son, and Deichtine helped to care for the newborn baby. As morning came, the house, the couple, and the child all vanished, leaving Deichtine and her companions confused. Even more mysteriously, Deichtine soon discovered that she was pregnant.

Deichtine returned to Emain Macha, the seat of Conchobar's kingdom, and was deeply troubled by the unexpected pregnancy. She told no one how it had happened, but over time it was revealed that the child she carried was special. In a dream, the god Lugh appeared to her and explained that it was he who had visited her in the form of the man from the house. The child she was carrying was his son, destined for greatness.

Deichtine gave birth to a son, whom she named Sétanta. From the moment of his birth, Sétanta displayed extraordinary strength and abilities far beyond those of an ordinary child. As he grew older, it became clear that he was destined for a great future. Sétanta trained as a warrior at Emain Macha and quickly gained a reputation for his bravery and skill.

One day, as a young boy, Sétanta was invited by his uncle, Conchobar, to a feast held by the blacksmith Culann. However, Sétanta was still playing sports with the other boys and promised to come later, making his way to the feast on his own. When Sétanta arrived at Culann's fort, the gates were closed, and Culann had released his fearsome guard dog, unaware that the boy had yet to arrive. As Sétanta approached, the massive hound attacked, but the boy fought back fiercely, and killed the dog. When Culann discovered what had happened, he was distraught, as the hound had been his protector. Sétanta, feeling responsible, offered to replace the hound by guarding Culann's property until a new dog could be trained. Impressed by the boy's bravery and sense of honor, Culann agreed.

From that day forward, Sétanta was known as Cú Chulainn, meaning "the Hound of Culann." His new name reflected the beginning of his journey as one of the greatest heroes in Irish mythology. Cú Chulainn's deeds would become legendary, but his birth and early life foretold the extraordinary destiny he was meant to fulfill.

Opposite: "Cuchulain slays the Hound of Culain," Chromolithograph from an illustration by Stephen Reid, from Eleanor Hull's *Cuchulain: The Hound of Ulster*, Harrap, London, 1909.

Left: "The young warrior Cuchulain sets out for Emain Macha, the capital of Ulster." Chromolithograph from a watercolor painting by Stephen Reid. From Eleanor Hull's *Cuchulain: The Hound of Ulster*, Harrap, London, 1909.

THE BOYHOOD DEEDS OF CÚ CHULAINN

From an early age, Cú Chulainn showed signs of greatness; even before he earned his famous name, his strength, courage, and skill in combat were unmatched.

He grew up at Emain Macha, the seat of King Conchobar mac Nessa, surrounded by the warriors of the Red Branch, but even among these renowned heroes, young Cú Chulainn stood out.

One day, when Cú Chulainn was only seven years old, he saw the boys of Emain Macha playing hurling together. Eager to join them, he asked his mother if he could go and play. She reluctantly agreed, but warned him to be cautious. Cú Chulainn, eager to prove himself, arrived at the playing field alone. As he approached, the boys did not welcome him at first—they saw him as too young and an outsider. However, Cú Chulainn was undeterred. In a show of strength, he entered the game, and without hesitation, defeated all of the boys, scoring multiple goals against them single-handedly.

The boys, furious at being bested, ganged up on Cú Chulainn, but they had underestimated his strength and skill. As they rushed him, Cú Chulainn fought them off, entering a wild battle frenzy known as a *ríastrad*, or warp-spasm. His body twisted and contorted in his fury, making him an unstoppable force. In the heat of battle, his appearance became monstrous, and none of the boys could stand against him. When King Conchobar arrived and saw the chaos, he intervened, calming Cú Chulainn and declaring him under his royal protection. From that moment on, the other boys welcomed him into their games, recognizing him as their equal—or even their superior.

Cú Chulainn's boyhood deeds continued to amaze the warriors of Ulster. On another occasion, while still just a child, he overheard a conversation about the famous warriors of the kingdom. They spoke of the great warrior Conall Cernach, who was given the champion's portion at every feast. When Cú Chulainn heard this, he became determined to earn his own place among the warriors.

At the age of just seven, Cú Chulainn took up arms. Though no one expected him to, he left Emain Macha and set out to find and defeat his enemies. He attacked the invading armies of the neighboring provinces, slaughtering dozens of warriors and bringing back their spoils to Ulster. His ferocity in battle stunned the warriors of the Red Branch, and they began to see that Cú Chulainn was no ordinary child—he was destined to be their greatest hero.

Among his many feats, one of the most famous occurred when Cú Chulainn defended the kingdom of Ulster from a band of warriors who had infiltrated its borders. Despite being vastly outnumbered, Cú Chulainn fought with such skill and fury that he drove the enemy back single-handedly. Afterward, he stood among the bodies of the fallen, his spear and shield drenched in blood, victorious yet again.

These early deeds of Cú Chulainn, as a mere boy, earned him great fame and established him as a future legend of Ireland. His bravery, battle prowess, and the strength of his character set him apart from all others.

CÚ CHULAINN AND SCÁTHACH

Cú Chulainn had become one of the most celebrated warriors of Ulster, but his heart longed for more than just glory in battle...

He was drawn to Emer—the daughter of Lord Forgall Monach—a woman known for her beauty, wisdom, and strong will. However, Emer was not easily won. She possessed the "six gifts of womanhood": beauty, a gentle voice, wisdom, needlework, chastity, and skill at speech, and her father was fiercely protective of her.

When Cú Chulainn first met Emer, he was immediately captivated by her grace and wit. The two exchanged words that were both sharp and playful, with Emer testing Cú Chulainn's resolve and worthiness. Though she was impressed by his reputation, Emer challenged Cú Chulainn, knowing that her father would not allow her to marry just any suitor. Forgall, too, was determined to prevent the match, fearing that Cú Chulainn's wild nature made him an unsuitable husband for his daughter.

Forgall, eager to dissuade the young warrior, devised a plan to keep them apart. He suggested that Cú Chulainn was not yet ready to marry Emer and that he should first undergo further training to become a truly great warrior. Forgall recommended that Cú Chulainn travel to the Isle of Skye, where he would be trained by Scáthach, the greatest warrior-woman and teacher of martial arts. The journey would be perilous, and the training even more so, but Cú Chulainn, undeterred by the challenge, agreed. Emer promised to wait for him, and Cú Chulainn swore that he would return to claim her hand.

Cú Chulainn set off on his journey to Skye, traveling across treacherous seas to reach Scáthach's fortress. Upon his arrival, he met the warrior-woman, who agreed to take him as her student. Scáthach's training was legendary, filled with intense trials and dangerous combat. She taught Cú Chulainn the use of weapons, advanced fighting techniques, and the secrets of the Gáe Bulg, a deadly spear that would become one of his most feared weapons.

During his time with Scáthach, Cú Chulainn encountered other warriors and faced many challenges. One of the most notable was the rivalry with Ferdiad, another pupil of Scáthach, with whom Cú Chulainn developed a strong bond of friendship. Though they would one day face each other in a tragic battle, during their time as students, they fought side by side, mastering the skills of war under Scáthach's tutelage.

At one point, Scáthach's rival, the fearsome warrior-woman Aífe, declared war against her. Cú Chulainn, loyal to his teacher, took up arms to defend Scáthach's honor and her land. During the battle, Cú Chulainn challenged Aífe to single combat. The two warriors fought fiercely, but Cú Chulainn, using both his strength and his cunning, gained the upper hand. He tricked Aífe by making her believe that her beloved chariot and horses had been destroyed, distracting her just long enough for him to disarm her. Cú Chulainn spared her life but demanded that Aífe make peace with Scáthach and grant her territory to her rival. She agreed to his terms, and peace was restored.

Impressed by his bravery and skill, Scáthach bestowed upon Cú Chulainn the final secrets of her warrior knowledge, completing his training. She foresaw that Cú Chulainn's destiny would be both glorious and tragic, and she warned him of the great challenges and sorrows that awaited him in the future.

Having completed his training, Cú Chulainn returned to Ireland, now a fully realized warrior of unmatched power and skill. Upon his return, he went straight to Forgall Monach's fortress to claim Emer as his bride. However, Forgall, still determined to prevent the marriage, refused and tried to have Cú Chulainn killed by setting his warriors upon him. But Forgall had gravely underestimated Cú Chulainn's strength. Cú Chulainn fought his way through the fortress, defeating Forgall's men with ease, scaling the walls, and finally confronting Forgall himself. In the end, Forgall fell to his death trying to escape, and Cú Chulainn carried Emer away, victorious.

Despite the violence and tragedy surrounding their courtship, Emer remained devoted to Cú Chulainn throughout his life. Their love story is one marked by trials and loyalty, with both partners demonstrating their strength and resilience. Cú Chulainn's time with Scáthach had made him a nearly unbeatable warrior, but his union with Emer showed that even the greatest of warriors sought companionship and love.

Right: Cú Chulainn is trained in the arts of fighting by Scáthach of the Shadows, seen here with her father. Illustration by Beatrice Elvery from *Heroes of the Dawn* by Violet Russell, 1914.

THE CURSE OF MACHA

The goddess Macha, a figure of great power and mystery, appeared one day in the house of Crunniuc, a wealthy farmer who had recently lost his wife...

Macha came without explanation and began living with Crunniuc, performing the duties of a wife and bringing prosperity to his household. She bore him children, and though her origins remained unknown, Crunniuc accepted her presence as a blessing.

One day, the king of Ulster, Conchobar mac Nessa, announced a great festival, and all the men of Ulster, including Crunniuc, were summoned to attend. Macha, heavily pregnant at the time, warned Crunniuc not to speak of her to anyone, especially the king. She urged him to attend quietly and return home without mentioning her.

However, during the festivities, Crunniuc, carried away by pride, boasted of his wife's abilities. He declared to the king and the assembled warriors that his wife could outrun the swiftest horses in the king's stable. Conchobar, intrigued and skeptical, demanded that Crunniuc prove his claim. Despite Crunniuc's pleas that his wife was near childbirth, the king's warriors seized him and sent for Macha, forcing her to compete in a race to defend her husband's boast.

Macha arrived, her belly heavy with child. She begged for mercy, asking to be allowed to give birth before being forced to race. The king and his men refused, mocking her and threatening Crunniuc's life if she did not comply. Seeing no escape, Macha reluctantly agreed.

When the race began, Macha ran with the speed of the wind, effortlessly outpacing the king's finest horses despite her condition. She crossed the finish line first, but at that very moment, she collapsed and gave birth to twins on the field. As she lay on the ground, her body wracked with pain, she turned to the men of Ulster and cursed them.

In her agony, Macha pronounced a powerful curse: in times of great need, when the men of Ulster were faced with their enemies, they would be struck with the same pain she had endured in childbirth. This curse would last for five days and five nights, rendering them helpless in the face of battle. Her words were imbued with supernatural force, and no man present could stop the curse from taking hold.

From that moment on, the men of Ulster were bound by Macha's curse. In times of crisis, when the province was under siege, they would fall to the ground, crippled by the unbearable pain of childbirth, leaving only the young and untested to defend the kingdom. The curse of Macha endured, becoming a central tragedy in the history of Ulster, leaving the province vulnerable at its most crucial moments.

Above: Conchobar mac Nessa, the High King of Ulster, Digitally-generated, courtesy of Brehon Academy; **Opposite:** *Macha Curses the Men of Ulster*, illustration by Stephen Reid, from *The Boys' Cuchulain* by Eleanor Hull, 1904

DEIDRE OF THE SORROWS

Deirdre, daughter of the royal storyteller Fedlimid mac Daill, was born under a dark prophecy...

Above: King Conchobar mac Nessa, High King of Ulster. Digitally-generated picture, courtesy of Brehon Academy; **Top:** Deirdre hugs the slain, bloody corpse of Naoise, her true love, killed by the treachery of Conchobar mac Nessa. Illustration by Helen Stratton, from *A Book of Myths*, 1915.

As Fedlimid celebrated the impending birth of his child at the court of Conchobar mac Nessa, High King of Ulster, a druid named Cathbad foretold that the girl would grow up to be the most beautiful woman in Ireland. But this beauty would bring disaster, death, and sorrow to the kingdom, leading to the downfall of many great warriors.

Despite the grim prophecy, Deirdre was born, and her fate was sealed. Fearing the prophecy, Conchobar decided to take control of Deirdre's destiny. He ordered that the infant be taken away and raised in isolation, under the care of a nurse named Leborcham, in a secluded place. Conchobar planned to keep Deirdre hidden until she was of age, at which point he would marry her himself, ensuring her beauty would belong to him and that the tragedy foretold would not unfold. Deirdre grew up in solitude, unaware of the outside world, but she blossomed into a woman of breathtaking beauty, just as the prophecy had foretold.

One winter day, as Deirdre looked out over the snow-covered landscape, she saw a raven feasting on the blood of a slain calf. Struck by the vivid contrast of the bird's black feathers, the red blood, and the white snow, she expressed a wish for a man who had the same colors: hair as black as the raven, skin as white as snow, and cheeks as red as blood. Her nurse, Leborcham, told her that such a man existed: Naoise, a young warrior of the Red Branch, and one of the three sons of Uisneach.

The more Deirdre learned of Naoise, the more she longed to meet him. Eventually,

fate brought them together. Naoise was as handsome and noble as Deirdre had imagined, and the two fell deeply in love. Knowing that Conchobar intended to claim her as his wife, Deirdre urged Naoise to flee with her, far from Ulster. Naoise, unable to resist Deirdre's plea, agreed, and together with his brothers, Ardan and Ainle, they escaped to Scotland.

For a time, Deirdre and Naoise lived happily in exile. The brothers of Uisneach and their companions found refuge with the king of Scotland, and Deirdre's beauty and charm brought them favor. But their happiness was not to last. Word of Deirdre's beauty reached Conchobar, and his desire for her had only grown during her absence. He hatched a plan to lure Naoise and his brothers back to Ulster. Conchobar sent Fergus mac Róich, a former king of Ulster and a man known for his honor, to bring the exiles home, promising them safe passage and a peaceful return.

Fergus, trusting in Conchobar's word, went to Scotland and persuaded Naoise and his brothers to return to Ulster. Deirdre, however, was filled with foreboding and did not trust Conchobar's promises. Despite her protests, Naoise and his brothers believed Fergus, and they began the journey back. When they arrived in Ulster, Fergus was called away to attend to other matters, leaving the brothers unprotected.

Upon their return, Conchobar's treachery was revealed. Instead of welcoming the brothers, Conchobar had them captured and imprisoned. He had Naoise and his brothers killed by Eogan mac Durthacht, one of his warriors. As Naoise fell, Deirdre's heart shattered. She was taken by Conchobar, who still intended to make her his wife despite the bloodshed that had unfolded.

For a year, Deirdre lived in Conchobar's court, but she was consumed by grief for Naoise. She refused to smile or speak, her beauty faded by the weight of her sorrow. Conchobar, frustrated by her refusal to love him, decided to further torment her by offering her as a prize to Eogan mac Durthacht, the man who had slain Naoise. On the way to Eogan's stronghold, Deirdre, seeing no escape from her misery, threw herself from the chariot onto a rock, ending her life.

Deirdre's death brought great sorrow to Ulster. Her beauty had indeed led to disaster, as foretold by the prophecy, and her love for Naoise had cost the lives of the sons of Uisneach and many others. Conchobar's actions, driven by his obsession with Deirdre, also led to discord within his kingdom. The warriors of the Red Branch were angered by his betrayal of the sons of Uisneach, and many of them, including Fergus mac Róich, left Ulster in disgust, joining the forces of Queen Medb of Connacht.

In death, Deirdre was reunited with Naoise. According to legend, their graves were placed side by side, and from each grew a tree that intertwined above them, forever entwining their souls despite the tragic circumstances of their lives.

Above: Fergus mac Róich, depicted in earlier, happy times, carrying Sétanta—who was to become Cú Chulainn, "the Hound of Ulster"—on his shoulder. Illustrated by George Denham, 1909, and from the *Irish Fairy Book*, edited by Alfred Perceval Graves, 1917; **Top:** Deirdre spent much of her early life in the care of her nurse, Leborcham. An illustration from *The Story of Deirdre* by John D. Batten, one of Joseph Jacob's collected stories in the book *Celtic Fairy Tales*, 1892; **Top, left:** Deirdre persuades her lover Naoise, together with his two brothers, Ardan and Ainle, to flee to Scotland. Another illustration by John D. Batten, and also from *The Story of Deirdre* in the same edition.

THE CATTLE RAID OF COOLEY

Queen Medb of Connacht, well-known amongst her people for her haughty pride and ambitions, sought to surpass her consort, Ailill, in wealth and power...

One evening, as they lay in bed, they began comparing their possessions. After tallying their riches—lands, treasures, and livestock—they discovered that Ailill owned a magnificent white-horned bull, the Finnbennach, which gave him an advantage. Determined to match him, Medb sought out a bull of equal or greater value.

She learned of a bull in the kingdom of Ulster, the Donn Cuailnge, a brown bull of extraordinary size and strength, owned by Dáire mac Fiachna. Medb decided she must have this bull to elevate her status. She sent messengers to Dáire, offering wealth and land in exchange for the Donn Cuailnge. At first, Dáire agreed to the deal, but when Medb's envoys boasted that they would take the bull by force if necessary, Dáire withdrew his offer.

Enraged by this insult, Medb prepared to invade Ulster and seize the bull. She assembled a massive army from across Ireland, calling upon the warriors of Connacht and her allies, including the fierce warrior Fergus mac Róich, once a king of Ulster but now an exile and ally of Connacht. Medb was confident of her success, for Ulster was under the curse of Macha, which left all the province's men incapacitated with labor pains at the moment of crisis. As we have seen, the curse had been laid upon when they had wronged the goddess Macha.

The only one unaffected by the curse was Cú Chulainn, the greatest warrior of Ulster, who was too young to have been bound by Macha's curse. As Medb's army advanced into Ulster, Cú Chulainn took it upon himself to defend the province. He employed the ancient custom of single combat, challenging one warrior at a time to fight him at the ford. Cú Chulainn, though only a youth, was unmatched in battle. He fought tirelessly, defeating each warrior sent against him, buying precious time for the men of Ulster to recover.

Medb, undeterred by the losses of her champions, continued her campaign. She sent Fergus mac Róich to parley with Cú Chulainn, hoping to convince him to yield. Fergus, once a mentor to Cú Chulainn, pleaded with him to abandon the fight, but Cú Chulainn refused. However, out of respect for Fergus, Cú Chulainn agreed to a temporary truce, during which Medb took the opportunity to push further into Ulster's territory.

Opposite: *Queen Maeve*, by J. C. Leyendecker, from *Myths and Legends of the Celtic Race*, 1911

Eventually, Queen Medb's army reached the lands of Cooley and captured the prized bull, Donn Cuailnge...

Above: Celtic Bull's Head, circa 5th-century BC, bronze. Like the people of the Minoan culture in Mediterranean Crete, bulls represented the mighty and virile aspects of nature and were an important symbol in the worship of a number of cults; **Top:** Queen Mebh with her prize, the magnificent Donn Cuailnge. Because of her hubris, a heavy price was paid by all. Digitally-generated image, courtesy Christine Dorman, moonfishwriting.com; **Opposite:** "Cuchulainn, chief hero of the Ultonians, carries Ferdiad across the river." Chromolithograph from a painting by E. Wallcousins, from *Celtic Myth and Legend* by Charles Squire, London 1900.

With the bull secured, Medb believed her victory was complete. However, Cú Chulainn continued to harass her army, killing many of her warriors and slowing her retreat back to Connacht. He faced one challenge after another, including battles with Ferdiad, his closest friend and foster brother, who was forced to fight him under Medb's orders.

The duel between Cú Chulainn and Ferdiad was one of the most tragic moments in the war. Bound by loyalty to opposing sides, the two warriors fought for three days at the ford. Though neither wished to kill the other, they were bound by honor to continue the fight. On the final day, Cú Chulainn unleashed the *Gáe Bolga*, a deadly spear technique he had learned from Scáthach. The spear mortally wounded Ferdiad, and Cú Chulainn, overcome with grief, cradled his dying friend in his arms.

After the death of Ferdiad, Cú Chulainn continued his lone defense of Ulster. The men of Ulster finally began to recover from the curse of Macha, and as they regained their strength, they rallied to join the fight. King Conchobar and his warriors emerged, ready to drive the invaders from their land.

The final battle was fierce, with both sides suffering heavy losses. Fergus mac Róich, still loyal to Medb, faced Conchobar on the battlefield. However, when Cú Chulainn appeared before him, Fergus chose to honor an old promise. In the past, when Fergus had been king of Ulster, Cú Chulainn had spared his life, and in return, Fergus had vowed never to fight him. Remembering this, Fergus withdrew from the battle, leading many of Medb's forces to retreat with him.

With Fergus's withdrawal, Medb's army crumbled. The warriors of Ulster pressed forward, defeating the remaining forces of Connacht. Medb, realizing the futility of further fighting, fled back to Connacht with her remaining troops, but she did not leave empty-handed. The Donn Cuailnge had been brought to Connacht, fulfilling her original goal of acquiring the prized bull.

However, the tale does not end there. In Connacht, Medb pitted the Donn Cuailnge against Ailill's white-horned bull, the

Finnbennach, hoping to prove her superiority over her husband once and for all. The two bulls clashed in a fierce and bloody battle that raged across the countryside, leaving devastation in their wake. The Donn Cuailnge, though stronger, was gravely injured in the fight. After killing the Finnbennach, the Donn Cuailnge wandered back to Ulster, bleeding and weakened. Upon reaching his home, the mighty bull collapsed and died from his wounds. In the end, Medb's quest for power and prestige was hollow. Though she had acquired the Donn Cuailnge and defeated her husband's bull, both animals were dead, and her invasion of Ulster had failed. The land of Ulster was left in ruins, but its people had survived, thanks to the heroism of Cú Chulainn.

THE DEATH OF CÚ CHULAINN

As Cú Chulainn grew older, his fame as the greatest warrior of Ulster spread throughout Ireland, but so did the hatred of his enemies.

His prowess in battle had won countless victories for Ulster, yet those victories had also bred deep resentment among the provinces of Connacht, Munster, and Leinster. Many sought to see him fall, and the time for their revenge would come.

Queen Medb of Connacht, who had already faced Cú Chulainn during the Cattle Raid of Cooley, still harbored a fierce grudge against him. She gathered her allies, including Lugaid mac Con Roí, the son of Cú Roí, a man whom Cú Chulainn had slain, and Erc, the son of Cairbre Nia Fer, another enemy of Ulster. Together, they formed a coalition with a singular purpose: to bring about the death of Cú Chulainn.

Cú Chulainn, knowing that his enemies were amassing forces against him, sensed that his final days were near. He had been warned by a series of omens. First, his trusted charioteer, Laeg, had seen three one-eyed hags washing his bloody armor in a river, a clear sign that death was approaching. Then, the Morrígan, the goddess of war and fate, appeared to him, revealing that the time of his death was at hand. Despite these warnings, Cú Chulainn faced his fate without fear, determined to meet his end in battle, as befitted a hero of his stature.

The enemies of Cú Chulainn devised a cunning plan to weaken him. They sent false messengers to Ulster, spreading word that a great force had gathered against the province, hoping to draw him out alone. As Cú Chulainn prepared to defend Ulster, he was confronted by a series of traps designed to sap his strength.

One of the final traps set by his enemies was a violation of his *geasa*, the magical taboos that bound Cú Chulainn's fate. One such *geas* forbade him from eating dog meat, as he was spiritually linked to the hound; another forbade him from refusing a gift of food from a woman. Knowing this, Lugaid and the sons of Calatin sent an old woman to offer Cú Chulainn a meal of roasted dog. Bound by his code, he was forced to eat the meat, and in doing so, his strength was severely diminished.

Weakened and aware that his time was near, Cú Chulainn nonetheless rode out to face his enemies, armed with his powerful spear, the *Gáe Bolga*. His loyal charioteer, Laeg, accompanied him, and they set off toward their fate. Along the way, Cú Chulainn faced numerous enemies, but despite his weakened state, he fought them off with the ferocity and skill that had made him legendary.

Opposite: *Cuchulain in Battle*, by J. C. Leyendecker. A raven of ill-omen accompanies Cú Chulainn and his trusted charioteer, Laeg, as they charge into battle. Illustration from *Myths and Legends of the Celtic Race*, 1911.

Left: Before his final battle, Cú Chulainn sees the raven of ill-omen. Chromolithograph from an illustration by Stephen Reid. Taken from Eleanor Hull's *Cuchulain: The Hound of Ulster*, 1909; **Opposite, left:** The Morrigan appears to Cú Chulainn. Early 20th-century, artist unknown; **Opposite, right:** After a mortal blow, Cú Chulainn ties himself to a standing stone with his own belt. Chromolithograph from an illustration by Stephen Reid. Taken from Eleanor Hull's *Cuchulain: The Hound of Ulster*, 1909.

In his final act of defiance, he tied himself to a standing stone with his own belt, determined to die on his feet, facing his enemies.

At last, Cú Chulainn came face to face with Lugaid mac Con Roí and Erc, who had gathered their forces for the final confrontation. The battle was fierce, but Cú Chulainn's strength had been greatly diminished by the curses and the tricks of his enemies.

During the fight, Lugaid hurled a spear that struck and killed Laeg, Cú Chulainn's faithful charioteer. Cú Chulainn, filled with grief but undeterred, continued to fight, though the odds were stacked against him.

At the height of the battle, Lugaid cast another spear, which struck Cú Chulainn in the stomach, gravely wounding him.

Despite the mortal blow, Cú Chulainn refused to fall. In his final act of defiance, he tied himself to a standing stone with his own belt, determined to die on his feet, facing his enemies.

There, as he stood bleeding, his enemies were too afraid to approach him, fearing that even in death, Cú Chulainn's power might destroy them.

For hours, Cú Chulainn stood against the stone, keeping his enemies at bay. Only when a raven, the symbol of the Morrígan, landed on his shoulder did they realize that he had finally died. Even in death, Cú Chulainn's legend persisted. Lugaid, hoping to claim victory, approached his body and attempted to cut off his head, but as he did, Cú Chulainn's sword fell from his lifeless hand and struck Lugaid, killing him instantly.

The men of Ulster, upon learning of Cú Chulainn's death, were overcome with grief. They retrieved his body and brought it back to Emain Macha, the royal seat of Ulster, where he was mourned as the greatest hero who had ever lived.

The death of Cú Chulainn marked the end of an era for Ulster, for no other warrior could match his skill, bravery, or devotion to his homeland.

THE FENIAN CYCLE

Above: Oisín, the son of Fionn mac Cumhaill, journeys to Tír na nÓg with Niamh of the Golden Hair, a princess from the Land of Eternal Youth. Illustration by Beatrice Elvery, in Violet Russell's *Heroes of the Dawn* of 1914.

The Fenian Cycle is the third of the four major cycles of Irish mythology, alongside the Mythological Cycle, the Ulster Cycle, and the Historical Cycle.

The Fenian Cycle primarily centers on the adventures of Fionn mac Cumhaill (also known as Finn MacCool) and his band of warriors, the Fianna, a legendary group of heroes known for their bravery, loyalty, and skill in battle. The Fenian Cycle is rich with tales of heroism, romance, and adventure, depicting a society deeply rooted in the warrior ethos, where personal honor, loyalty to one's comrades, and courage in the face of danger are paramount.

Set during a time when Ireland was ruled by a High King, the Fenian Cycle's stories are primarily concerned with the exploits of the Fianna, who served as a standing army protecting the kingdom. Unlike the Ulster Cycle, which focuses more on kings and the political struggles between provinces, the Fenian Cycle emphasizes the lives and adventures of the warrior class, with Fionn mac Cumhaill as their leader. The Fianna were not only fierce warriors but also poets, hunters, and scholars, embodying the ideal of a well-rounded hero.

THE FIANNA

The Fianna were a group of elite warriors, serving both as protectors of the High King of Ireland and as a roaming band of adventurers. They were known for their skills in battle, their loyalty to each other, and their role as hunters and defenders of the land. Life within the Fianna was governed by strict codes of honor, and only the most skilled and brave could join their ranks. Membership was open to warriors of all backgrounds, provided they could meet the demanding physical and mental challenges.

The Fianna lived a life of freedom, roaming the forests and hills of Ireland, often independent of the king's court. They were deeply connected to nature, spending much of their time hunting and living off the land. While the Fianna were loyal to the king, they were also a powerful force in their own right, and their allegiance was often tested by shifting political landscapes and personal rivalries.

The stories of the Fenian Cycle explore several key themes, including loyalty, honor, and the transient nature of life. The Fianna, though heroic and powerful, are ultimately doomed to fall. Many of the cycle's tales reflect the tension between the glory of battle and the inevitable decline of even the greatest warriors. Tragic love stories, such as the doomed romance between Diarmuid and Gráinne, also play a significant role in the cycle, highlighting the emotional cost of heroism and loyalty.

MAJOR TALES

The Fenian Cycle includes numerous well-known tales. One of the most famous is The Pursuit of Diarmuid and Gráinne, which tells the story of Diarmuid, a member of the Fianna, and Gráinne, the betrothed of Fionn. Gráinne falls in love with Diarmuid and compels him to flee with her, leading to a long chase across Ireland as they are pursued by Fionn and his warriors. Despite Fionn's eventual forgiveness, Diarmuid's fate is sealed when he is mortally wounded by a boar, and Fionn's delayed healing ultimately causes Diarmuid's death.

Another notable tale is The Battle of Gabhra, which marks the end of the Fianna. In this battle, the Fianna are betrayed, leading to their downfall and the death of many of Fionn's greatest warriors, including his grandson, Oscar. The battle serves as the culmination of the cycle's theme of the decline of the heroic age.

Above: "Finn came to the aid of the weary Fianna," illustration by Stephen Reid, from *The High Deeds of Finn and other Bardic Romances of Ancient Ireland*, by Thomas Rolleston, 1910; **Top left:** The Fianna, an illustration by Arthur Rackham from *Irish Fairy Tales*, 1920; **Top right:** "The Fianna raised a pillar stone..." another illustration by Stephen Reid, from *The Myths & Legends of the Celtic Race* by Thomas Rolleston, 1911

NOTABLE FIGURES

Above: *Ossian evoking ghosts at the edge of the Lora*, by François Gérard, painted for Napoleon Bonaparte in 1801. "Ossian" is the Scottish version of the Irish hero Oisín, and more than likely a name devised by Scots author James Macpherson in 1761. Macpherson's epic poem became internationally famous and his invented character "Fingal" was loosely based on...Oisín's father—Fionn mac Cumhaill. In the painting, Ossian is the harp player in the bottom left corner, and the other characters in the picture depict the people from his now distant past, with the central character being Fingal, Ossian's father. Oisin's journey to Tír na nÓg with Niamh, and his tragic return—and which the narrative of this painting references, calls one back to the truth of the human condition contained in these ancient stories.

FIONN MAC CUMHAILL

Fionn mac Cumhaill is the central figure of the Fenian Cycle. He is the leader of the Fianna, a band of warriors renowned for their skill, bravery, and loyalty.

Fionn's wisdom is legendary, gained after he ate the Salmon of Knowledge, a magical fish that imparted great insight. With this wisdom, Fionn became not only a formidable warrior but also a man of deep understanding and leadership.

His role as the protector of Ireland and his connection to both the natural and supernatural worlds make him one of the most beloved heroes of Irish mythology. He is a multifaceted character, equally skilled in battle and in matters of the heart, but his life is also marked by personal tragedies, including the death of his father, Cumhall, and the loss of his beloved warriors.

OISÍN

Oisín, Fionn's son, is a warrior-poet whose name is synonymous with both heroism and artistry.

Known for his strength in battle, Oisín is also celebrated for his poetic abilities, representing the ideal of the warrior-poet. One of the most famous tales involving Oisín is his love story with Niamh of the Golden Hair, a woman from the Otherworld. Oisín travels with her to Tír na nÓg, the land of eternal youth, where they live together for centuries. However, Oisín eventually longs to return to Ireland, only to find that hundreds of

years have passed, and the Ireland he knew is long gone. His tragic return to the mortal world, where he ages rapidly, and is condemned to tell the old tales of bravery and heroism from a time that has passed, symbolizes the tension between the eternal and the transient that runs throughout the Fenian Cycle.

DIARMUID UA DUIBHNE

Diarmuid Ua Duibhne is one of the most tragic heroes of the Fenian Cycle.

Known for his incredible beauty and charm, Diarmuid is gifted with a magical "love spot" on his forehead that causes women to fall instantly in love with him.

This gift, however, also leads to his tragic fate. Diarmuid's most famous story is The Pursuit of Diarmuid and Gráinne, in which Gráinne, the betrothed of Fionn mac Cumhaill, falls in love with Diarmuid and convinces him to elope with her. The couple is pursued by Fionn and the Fianna across Ireland. Though Fionn eventually forgives Diarmuid, the hero is later killed by a boar during a hunting expedition. Despite his fatal wounds, Diarmuid could have been saved by Fionn's healing powers, but Fionn, out of lingering resentment, delays the aid, leading to Diarmuid's death.

OSCAR

Oscar is the grandson of Fionn mac Cumhaill and one of the fiercest warriors of the Fianna.

As the son of Oisín, Oscar inherits his father's strength and heroism and plays a major role in many of the Fenian Cycle's battles. His most significant act of bravery occurs during The Battle of Gabhra, the climactic fight that marks the downfall of the Fianna. Oscar dies heroically in battle, marking the end of an era for the Fianna, and his death is deeply mourned by Fionn.

GOLL MAC MORNA

Goll mac Morna is another significant figure in the Fenian Cycle, known for his leadership of the Fianna before Fionn's rise to power.

Goll was responsible for the death of Fionn's father, Cumhall, which created a lasting tension between him and Fionn. However, despite this enmity, Goll and Fionn often fought side by side against common enemies. Goll is portrayed as both an honorable and tragic figure, a warrior who represents the old guard of the Fianna, and his complex relationship with Fionn is a key element of the cycle's stories.

Top left: Fionn mac Cumhaill confronted by the fearsome demon Aillén in the frontispiece to Violet Russell's *Heroes of the Dawn* of 1914. Illustration by Beatrice Elvery; **Top right:** Goll mac Morna, sourced from Irish Heritage News

THE SALMON OF KNOWLEDGE

Long ago in Ireland, there was a prophecy that foretold the existence of the Salmon of Knowledge, a magical fish that would grant all the knowledge of the world to whoever consumed its flesh.

Above: Digital illustration introducing *The Salmon of Knowledge*, courtesy of Meet the Myths; **Opposite, top:** Finegas, the druid poet, sits at the Well of Wisdom, *an Tobar Segais*, the secret pool close to the River Boyne, patiently fishing for the Salmon of Knowledge. Courtesy of Tomás Ó Cárthaigh at writingsinrhyme.co; **Opposite, bottom:** An AI-generated depiction of the young Fionn mac Cumhaill and the key elements of the tale—the hazelnut tree, and of course, the magical Salmon. Courtesy of Meet the Myths.

The salmon lived in a secret pool, fed by the hazelnuts that fell from the nine sacred hazel trees growing around it. The wisdom contained in the hazelnuts made the salmon a creature of immense power, and many sought to catch it, hoping to gain its knowledge.

One such man was Finegas, a wise old poet and druid who had dedicated his life to seeking the Salmon of Knowledge. He lived by the River Boyne, near the secret pool where the salmon was said to reside, and spent years fishing in its waters, always hoping to catch the fabled fish. Despite his wisdom and persistence, Finegas had never been able to catch the salmon, though he never gave up his quest.

At that time, a young boy named Fionn mac Cumhaill came to study under Finegas. Fionn was the son of Cumhall, a great warrior who had been killed when Fionn was very young. Fionn had been raised in secret, trained by warrior women, and had become skilled in combat and knowledge, but he sought to gain wisdom from the learned poet Finegas. Finegas took Fionn as his pupil, teaching him the ways of poetry and the secrets of nature.

One day, after many years of trying, Finegas finally caught the Salmon of Knowledge. He was overjoyed, for he knew that consuming the salmon would grant him the wisdom he had long sought. He instructed Fionn to cook the fish for him, but he warned the boy not to taste even a single bite. Finegas wanted to be the one to gain the knowledge, as he had spent his life searching for the salmon.

Fionn obeyed his teacher and began to cook the fish over the fire. However, as he was turning the fish, a drop of hot oil from the salmon splashed onto Fionn's thumb, burning him. Without thinking, Fionn put his thumb in his mouth to ease the pain. In that moment, all the wisdom of the world flooded into him. Fionn had unintentionally gained the knowledge of the Salmon of Knowledge.

When Fionn brought the cooked salmon to Finegas, the poet noticed something had changed in the boy. He asked if Fionn had tasted any of the fish, and Fionn explained what had happened. Realizing that the prophecy had been fulfilled, and that Fionn was destined to receive the knowledge, Finegas accepted his fate. He told Fionn that the knowledge now belonged to him and that he would go on to become a great and wise leader.

With the wisdom he had gained from the Salmon of Knowledge, Fionn grew into the legendary leader of the Fianna, the greatest band of warriors in Ireland. His strength, bravery, and newfound wisdom guided him through many adventures, and he became one of the most revered figures in Irish mythology. From that day on, whenever Fionn needed wisdom, he would place his thumb in his mouth, and the knowledge he had gained from the salmon would flow into him once more.

One day, while out hunting with his warriors, Fionn mac Cumhaill came across a beautiful doe in the forest. This was no ordinary deer—her graceful movements and striking appearance caught Fionn's attention immediately...

Above: Detail of a sketch for *Sadhbh*, by Arthur Rackham, 1910, Sourced from *Gypsy Monika's blog*; **Top:** The beautiful doe was Sadhbh, a woman cursed by the evil druid Fer Doirich to wander the forest in the form of a deer

He and his hounds gave chase, but the doe moved with incredible speed, always staying just out of reach. Eventually, Fionn's magical hounds, Bran and Sceólang, who had been born from a human woman and had powers of their own, sensed something strange about the deer and refused to harm her. Fionn, realizing that there was magic at play, stopped the chase and let the doe live.

That night, the doe appeared again, but this time she did not flee. Instead, she approached Fionn, and as he gazed at her, she transformed into a beautiful woman before his eyes. Her name was Sadhbh, and she explained her tragic story. Sadhbh had once been a human woman, but she had been cursed by the evil druid Fer Doirich, who was furious when she refused to marry him. As punishment, he turned her into a doe and left her to wander the forests in animal form. The only way the curse could be broken was if she entered the lands of Fionn mac Cumhaill, for Fer Doirich's magic held no power there.

Now free from the curse, Sadhbh revealed that she had been drawn to Fionn because of his great reputation as a noble and just leader. Over time, the two fell deeply in love, and they were soon married. Sadhbh and Fionn lived happily together for a time, and their love blossomed. Sadhbh became

FIONN AND SADHBH

pregnant, and Fionn eagerly awaited the birth of their child. He had finally found peace and happiness after years of leading the Fianna in battles and adventures.

However, their joy was not to last. One day, while Fionn was away from their home, Fer Doirich returned, still furious that Sadhbh had escaped his curse. Using his dark magic, he tricked Sadhbh by creating the illusion of Fionn outside the house. Thinking her husband had returned, Sadhbh ran out to meet him, only to be confronted by Fer Doirich. Before she could react, he transformed her back into a doe and whisked her away from Fionn's lands.

When Fionn returned and discovered that Sadhbh had disappeared, he was devastated. He searched the forests and mountains for her, but she was nowhere to be found. Despite his best efforts, Fionn could not undo the druid's dark magic. Sadhbh was lost to him forever.

Though Sadhbh was gone, she had left behind a son. In the wilderness, Sadhbh had given birth to a boy, who was later found and brought to Fionn. The child was named Oisín, and he would grow up to be one of the greatest warriors and poets of the Fianna, continuing his father's legacy. Fionn never forgot Sadhbh, and though he found happiness with his son, the loss of his beloved wife remained a source of sorrow for the rest of his days.

Above: "Follow me now to the Hill of Allen..." Fionn and Sadhbh, for a while happy and content... an illustration by Stephen Reid, from *The High Deeds of Finn and other Bardic Romances of Ancient Ireland*, by Thomas Rolleston, 1910

FIONN AND AILLÉN

In the time when Fionn mac Cumhaill was a young warrior, Ireland faced a terrible threat each year during the festival of Samhain.

Above: "Finn heard far off the first notes of the fairy harp." An illustration by Stephen Reid from *The High Deeds of Finn and other Bardic Romances of Ancient Ireland* by Thomas Rolleston, 1910; **Opposite:** Fionn mac Cumhaill fighting Aillén by Beatrice Elvery, in Violet Russell's *Heroes of the Dawn* of 1914

A fire-breathing demon named Aillén mac Midhna would come from the Otherworld to the Hill of Tara, the seat of the High King. Each year, Aillén would play his magical harp, lulling the warriors of Tara into a deep sleep, and then he would burn the palace to the ground with his fiery breath. No one had been able to stop him, and for years, Tara was left defenseless.

At this time, Fionn mac Cumhaill was not yet the leader of the Fianna, the band of warriors who protected Ireland. He had been training under his mentor Finegas and had gained great knowledge and skill. Eager to prove himself and avenge the death of his father, Cumhall, who had once been the leader of the Fianna, Fionn sought a way to stop Aillén and save Tara.

The king, Cormac mac Airt, and his warriors were preparing for another Samhain, dreading the inevitable destruction. Fionn arrived at Tara and offered his help, but the king and his men doubted the abilities of this young warrior. However, Fionn was determined and asked for the chance to face Aillén. Knowing the demon's power to put his enemies to sleep, Fionn sought the aid of a magical item—a special spear that had been enchanted to keep its wielder awake and alert.

When the night of Samhain arrived, Aillén appeared once more, ready to destroy Tara as he had done for many years. He began to play his magical harp, and as expected, the warriors of Tara fell into a deep sleep. But Fionn, holding his enchanted spear tightly, remained unaffected by the music's spell. When Aillén finished his song and prepared to unleash his fiery breath on Tara, Fionn acted quickly. A fierce battle ensued, but Fionn's speed and skill with the spear were unmatched. With one powerful throw, Fionn struck Aillén, killing him and saving Tara from destruction. The long-standing curse of Aillén's attacks was finally broken.

When the warriors of Tara awoke and realized what had happened, they were amazed by Fionn's bravery and skill. King Cormac, seeing that Fionn was truly his father's son and a warrior of great ability, welcomed him as a hero. To honor his victory, Fionn was granted leadership of the Fianna, the role once held by his father.

B.

THE GIANT'S CAUSEWAY

Fionn was a great warrior and leader of the Fianna, but he was also known for his incredible size and strength. Across the sea in Scotland lived a giant named Benandonner, who was just as large and powerful.

The two had never met, but they often taunted each other from across the waters, boasting of their strength and daring one another to fight.

Benandonner, confident in his own abilities, mocked Fionn from the Scottish shores, challenging him to a battle to prove who was the strongest giant. Fionn, tired of the insults and eager to defend his honor, decided to take up the challenge.

But there was a problem—the sea between Ireland and Scotland was too wide to cross easily. Not one to be discouraged, Fionn came up with a plan to reach his rival.

Using his immense strength, Fionn began to pick up massive stones from the coast of Ireland. He hurled them into the sea, one by one, creating a path of giant stepping stones that would stretch all the way to Scotland. This causeway would allow him to walk across the water and confront Benandonner face-to-face.

As Fionn neared the completion of his task, he began to feel the weight of the upcoming battle. Benandonner was known to be a fearsome giant, and Fionn wasn't sure if he could defeat him. As he prepared to cross the causeway, he shared his

concerns with his wife, Oonagh, who was clever and quick-witted. She reassured him that she had a plan.

Before Fionn could face Benandonner, Oonagh disguised him as a baby, wrapping him in blankets and placing him in a giant cradle. When Benandonner arrived in Ireland, having crossed the causeway Fionn had built, he found Oonagh at home but saw no sign of Fionn. Oonagh welcomed him in, pretending Fionn was away, but invited him to meet their "child"—the disguised Fionn.

When Benandonner saw the enormous "baby" in the cradle, he was stunned. If this was Fionn's child, he thought, then Fionn himself must be a giant beyond comprehension. Fearful of facing such a massive opponent, Benandonner quickly retreated, terrified of the strength Fionn must possess.

As he fled back across the causeway to Scotland, Benandonner destroyed the path behind him, tearing up the stones so that Fionn could not follow. Only the remnants of the causeway remained, scattered in the sea.

Opposite, top: A digitally-generated portrait of Fionn mac Cumhaill, courtesy of the brehonacademy.org; **Above and opposite, below:** The Giant's Causeway in County Antrim, Northern Ireland—the remains of Fionn mac Cumhaill's stepping stones to Scotland. Alternately, geologists have it that the Giant's Causeway first began to form around 60 million years ago, when the British Isles and Europe were still attached to the North American continent. Europe and North America began to move apart, creating great cracks in the earth's crust. Through those cracks rose a great outpouring of lava and molten rock, which upon cooling on the chalk substrata produced the signature hexagonal rods of basalt which amaze us today. The Giant's Causeway is a World Heritage Site, protected and cared for by the National Trust of the United Kingdom and is at 44 Causeway Road, Bushmills, County Antrim, BT57 8SU.

OISÍN'S JOURNEY TO TÍR NA NÓG

One day, as Oisín, the son of Fionn mac Cumhaill, was out hunting with the Fianna, a beautiful woman riding a white horse appeared before them. Her golden hair flowed in the wind, and she was dressed in shimmering, otherworldly garments...

Oisín and the other warriors were struck by her beauty. The woman introduced herself as Niamh of the Golden Hair, a princess from Tír na nÓg, the Land of Eternal Youth. She had come to find Oisín, having heard of his great deeds and noble heart, and she invited him to travel with her to her magical homeland.

Niamh described Tír na nÓg as a paradise where no one aged, and no one knew sickness or death. Oisín, enchanted by her beauty and the promise of this idyllic place, agreed to go with her, leaving behind his father, Fionn, and the Fianna. He climbed onto Niamh's magical horse, and as soon as they set off, the horse galloped across the sea, carrying them toward Tír na nÓg.

Upon arriving in Tír na nÓg, Oisín was welcomed with great joy. The land was indeed as beautiful as Niamh had promised—its people lived in eternal youth, and there was no sorrow or suffering. Oisín and Niamh fell deeply in love, and for what seemed like a short time, they lived together happily. Oisín felt as though only a few years had passed, but time in Tír na nÓg flowed differently from the mortal world.

Despite the beauty and peace of Tír na nÓg, Oisín began to long for his homeland and wished to visit Ireland to see his father, Fionn, and the Fianna once more. Niamh warned him that many years had passed in Ireland since he left, and that returning to the mortal world could be dangerous. However, she agreed to let him go, giving him her magical horse for the journey. She warned him never to dismount from the horse, for if his feet touched the ground, he would not be able to return to Tír na nÓg.

Oisín set out for Ireland, and when he arrived, he was shocked by what he found. The Fianna were gone, and Ireland had changed drastically. He asked the people he encountered if they knew of Fionn mac Cumhaill or the Fianna, but no one recognized the names. Hundreds of years had passed in Ireland since Oisín had left, though it had felt like only a few years to him.

As Oisín rode through the countryside, he came across a group of men struggling to lift a large stone. Wanting to help, Oisín bent down from his horse and lifted the stone with ease. However, as he did so, the saddle broke, and he fell to the ground. The moment his feet touched the earth, Niamh's warning came true. Oisín's youthful appearance vanished, and he aged rapidly, becoming an old man in an instant.

Oisín never returned to Tír na nÓg. He remained in Ireland, an old man with memories of the Fianna and the Land of Eternal Youth, telling the stories of his adventures to the people he met, keeping alive the legends of his father and his own journey to the magical land beyond the sea.

Above: Oisín and Niamh arrive in Tír na nÓg—the Land of Eternal Youth—on Niamh's magical steed. Illustration by Stephen Reid from *Myths & Legends of the Celtic Race* by Thomas Rolleston, 1911.

Above: The betrothal party of Gráinne to Fionn mac Cumhaill. Grainne has noticed Diamuid, a handsome warrior of the Fianna. Illustration by Henry Justice Ford, from *The Book of Romance*, 1902, edited by Andrew Lang; **Opposite:** Diarmuid and Gráinne in the "Quicken Tree," also illustrated by Henry Justice Ford, again from *The Book of Romance*.

At the feast celebrating their betrothal, Gráinne's eyes fell on Diarmuid Ua Duibhne, a handsome warrior of the Fianna, known for his charm and bravery. Diarmuid bore a magical love spot on his forehead, which made him irresistible to women, and Gráinne found herself drawn to him.

Determined not to marry Fionn, Gráinne hatched a plan. She slipped a sleeping potion into the drinks of the guests at the feast, sending everyone except Diarmuid into a deep slumber. She then approached Diarmuid and confessed her love for him, demanding that he run away with her. Diarmuid, loyal to Fionn and aware of the consequences of betraying his leader, refused. However, Gráinne placed him under *geis*, a binding magical obligation, to take her with him. Bound by this powerful *geis*, Diarmuid had no choice but to flee with Gráinne.

Thus began the Pursuit of Diarmuid and Gráinne, as Fionn, enraged by their betrayal, vowed to hunt them down. Accompanied by the Fianna, Fionn pursued the couple across Ireland. Diarmuid and Gráinne traveled through forests, over mountains, and across rivers, always managing to stay one step ahead of their pursuers. Along the way, they found shelter in various places, but they were constantly on the move, never able to rest for long.

Despite his initial reluctance, Diarmuid grew to love Gráinne as they journeyed together. His loyalty to Fionn was strong, but his love for Gráinne became even stronger. They endured many hardships as they tried to evade Fionn's relentless pursuit. Diarmuid's comrades in the Fianna, many of whom respected and admired him, often found themselves torn between their loyalty to Fionn and their sympathy for Diarmuid. Some of them secretly helped Diarmuid and Gráinne during their flight, providing them with shelter or supplies.

THE PURSUIT OF DIARMUID AND GRÁINNE

Gráinne, the beautiful daughter of the High King of Ireland, Cormac mac Airt, was promised in marriage to the great warrior Fionn mac Cumhaill, leader of the Fianna. Although Fionn was a renowned hero, he was now an old man, and Gráinne, young and spirited, did not wish to marry him...

Eventually, Diarmuid and Gráinne managed to find refuge with Aengus Óg, the god of love and Diarmuid's foster father. Aengus offered them protection, and for a time, the couple was safe from Fionn's wrath. Over the years, the intensity of Fionn's pursuit began to fade, and Diarmuid and Gráinne were able to live peacefully together. They settled down, and Gráinne bore Diarmuid several children.

However, the story does not end well. Years later, Fionn and Diarmuid were brought together during a boar hunt. Diarmuid, despite his great skill as a warrior, was fatally gored by a wild boar. As Diarmuid lay dying, Fionn had the chance to save him by offering him water from his hands, which held healing powers. But Fionn, still bitter over Diarmuid's betrayal, hesitated for too long, and by the time he brought the water, Diarmuid was dead.

Gráinne was left heartbroken, mourning the loss of the man she had risked everything to be with, while Fionn, despite his revenge, was left with the bitterness of losing both a trusted warrior and a love he had never fully won.

THE BATTLE OF GABHRA

The Battle of Gabhra, said to have taken place sometime between 283 AD and 296 AD, was one of the most tragic and decisive conflicts in the history of the Fianna, marking the end of their era as the greatest warriors in Ireland.

Above: Goll mac Morna, once a Fianna warrior but now an ally of Caibre Lifechair, the High King of Ireland. Sourced from Irish Heritage News

Tensions had been building for some time between the Fianna and the High King of Ireland, Cairbre Lifechair, who had grown wary of their power and influence. Fionn mac Cumhaill and his warriors had long protected the land, but their strength had become a threat to the king's authority.

These tensions eventually boiled over into open conflict, leading to the battle that would bring the Fianna to their tragic end. The conflict began when Cairbre insulted the Fianna by refusing to pay them the tribute they had traditionally received for their service. Cairbre's refusal was a direct challenge to the Fianna's honor, and the warriors, led by Oscur, Fionn's grandson, were enraged.

Oscur, known for his bravery and fierce loyalty to the Fianna, took up arms to defend their honor. However, the aging Fionn did not lead the Fianna into this final battle, as he was no longer the active leader of the group.

Oscur and the Fianna found themselves facing Cairbre's forces on the battlefield at Gabhra. Cairbre had enlisted the help of former Fianna warriors who had grown resentful of Fionn's leadership, including Goll mac Morna, a once-strong ally of the Fianna but now a bitter rival. The battle was fierce and bloody, with both sides suffering heavy losses.

The warriors of the Fianna fought valiantly, but they were outnumbered and weary. In the heart of the battle, Oscur clashed with Cairbre himself. The fight between the two was intense, and Oscur, though young and strong, was mortally wounded by the king's spear. With his last ounce of strength, Oscur struck Cairbre down, killing him before succumbing to his own wounds. Oscur's death was a devastating blow to the Fianna, as he was one of their most powerful and beloved warriors.

The losses continued to mount, and as the battle raged on, the Fianna were gradually overwhelmed. Many of Fionn's greatest warriors fell that day, and the legendary band was nearly destroyed. Although the Fianna fought with unmatched skill and bravery, their time had passed, and the era of their dominance came to an end on the field at Gabhra.

"O Oscur, light of my eyes, child of my heart, would that I were lying in your place," lamented Fionn...

When Fionn saw Oscur, dying on the battlefield, he was heartbroken. The loss of his grandson, along with so many of his comrades, marked the end of an era. Though Fionn had survived the battle, his heart was heavy with grief, and he would never again lead the Fianna into battle. The once-great band of warriors, who had defended Ireland for generations, was shattered, and the battle of Gabhra became a symbol of the fall of the Fianna.

Left: Fionn discovers his grandson Oscur, waiting for death on the battlefield of Gabhra. Illustration by Beatrice Elvery from "The Death of Oscur" in *Heroes of the Dawn*, 1914, by Violet Russell.

THE HISTORICAL CYCLE

The Historical Cycle, also called the Cycle of the Kings, is the fourth of the major cycles of Irish mythology. Unlike the other cycles that focus on gods, heroes, and warriors, the Historical Cycle is primarily concerned with the legendary kings of Ireland and the events surrounding their reigns. These stories blend history, myth, and folklore to give semi-historical accounts of Ireland's royal past, focusing on themes of leadership, justice, and the relationship between rulers and the divine.

Above: "Conary in the Toils of the Fairy Folk." Conaire Mor, or Conary, one of the legendary High Kings of Ireland, from a watercolor by Stephen Reid, circa 1909

KINGSHIP AND MYTH

The kings in the Historical Cycle are portrayed as both mortal rulers and figures of symbolic importance. Their reigns are often shaped by interactions with supernatural forces, suggesting that kingship itself was seen as divinely influenced. These stories explore the responsibilities of rulers, portraying them as protectors of the land whose actions could either bring prosperity or devastation. A key element of the cycle is the idea that a king's moral and ethical choices directly affected the health and stability of his kingdom. The relationship between kings and their subjects is central to many of the tales. The king was expected to uphold justice, fairness, and honor. A righteous ruler would be rewarded with peace and prosperity, while a corrupt or unjust king would bring chaos and suffering to his people. The balance between personal ambition and the broader welfare of the kingdom is a recurring theme in the cycle, often highlighting the difficult choices that come with leadership.

THEMES OF SACRED KINGSHIP

One of the primary themes of the Historical Cycle is the concept of sacred kingship, where the ruler's authority is closely tied to divine will and the fertility of the land. A king who adhered to the laws of the gods, respected sacred taboos (*geasa*), and ruled wisely would ensure the well-being of his kingdom. However, when a king broke these divine laws or failed to fulfill his duties, his reign would be marked by disaster and upheaval. This connection between the king's actions and the fate of the land reflects a deep cultural belief in the sacred nature of rulership in ancient Ireland.

Another important theme in the Historical Cycle is the idea of fate and prophecy. Many of the stories feature kings whose destinies were foretold by druids or supernatural beings. These prophecies often shaped the lives and reigns of the kings, with some fulfilling their fates heroically while others met tragic ends. The influence of fate in these tales emphasizes the role of the divine in determining the course of leadership and the success or failure of a king's rule.

POWER AND LEADERSHIP

The stories of the Historical Cycle often highlight the challenges of leadership, exploring the complexities of power and the relationships between kings and their people. Kings are portrayed not only as warriors but also as lawmakers, responsible for maintaining order and justice in their realms. Their ability to balance these roles, often in the face of internal strife or external threats, is a key aspect of their reigns.

Opposite: *Sencha the Druid on the Hill of Slane*. Chromolithograph from a Stephen Reid illustration of 1909. The Historical Cycle features kings whose destinies have been foretold by druids...

NOTABLE FIGURES

The Historical Cycle of Irish mythology centers on the legendary kings of Ireland and their interactions with both the divine and mortal realms...

Above: Nemglan, a deity from the Land of Eternal Youth, visits Mess Búachalla, the wife of Eterscél, the High King of Ireland. Subsequently, Mess Búachalla conceives their son...Conaire Mór, (or Conary.) Illustration by Stephen Reid, circa 1909.

These rulers are often depicted as larger-than-life figures whose reigns were marked by significant events, decisions, and moral dilemmas. Some of the most notable kings in this cycle include Cormac mac Airt, Conaire Mór, and Niall of the Nine Hostages, each of whom played a crucial role in shaping the narratives of Irish myth and history.

CORMAC MAC AIRT

One of the most celebrated kings of the Historical Cycle is Cormac mac Airt, who is often portrayed as the ideal ruler. He was a High King of Ireland and ruled from the Hill of Tara, the traditional seat of power for Irish kings. Cormac was known for his wisdom, justice, and fairness, and his reign was seen as a golden age of prosperity.

According to legend, Cormac was responsible for codifying ancient Irish law, including the Bretha Nemed Toísech, a system of laws that helped maintain social order. Cormac's sense of justice and his ability to balance power with compassion made him a revered figure in Irish lore. His leadership is often held up as a model of what a king should strive to be.

Cormac's reign is also filled with stories of supernatural encounters and challenges. In one tale, he is given a magical cup that would break if lies were spoken in its presence, symbolizing his commitment to truth and fairness. Cormac's wisdom even extended into his dealings with the gods, and he was often portrayed as a king who sought to bridge the worlds of mortals and the divine.

CONAIRE MÓR

Conaire Mór is another prominent figure in the Historical Cycle, and his story serves as a powerful example of the consequences of breaking sacred taboos. Conaire was a High King of Ireland who came to power under auspicious

circumstances, with divine support and the promise of a prosperous reign. However, Conaire was bound by a series of *geasa*—rules or prohibitions that he was forbidden to break. These taboos were not only personal but were tied to the well-being of his kingdom.

Despite his initial success, Conaire's reign took a tragic turn when he unknowingly broke several of his *geasa*. This led to chaos and destruction in his kingdom, and ultimately to his own death. Conaire's story highlights the delicate balance between divine law and mortal power, and the inevitable consequences of ignoring fate and sacred obligations.

NIALL OF THE NINE HOSTAGES

Niall of the Nine Hostages is a semi-historical figure from the Historical Cycle whose legacy had a lasting impact on Ireland. Niall was a powerful High King, known for his military campaigns and his role in consolidating power across the island. His name comes from the practice of taking hostages from rival kingdoms as a means of securing peace and loyalty. Niall's exploits took him far beyond Ireland, and he is said to have raided across Britain and even into mainland Europe.

Niall's descendants, the Uí Néill dynasty, became one of the most influential families in Irish history, dominating the political landscape for centuries. His reign marked the beginning of a new era in Irish leadership, with his legacy extending beyond myth into recorded history.

Above: Portrait of Niall Noígíallach, sourced from Celtic Native; **Top, and opposite top:** The Hill of Tara, from where the High King of Ireland ruled. It's a mystical landscape which held deep spiritual resonance for Irish Celts, and even today its awesome presence exerts a strong pull.

THE MADNESS OF KING SWEENEY

King Sweeney (also known as *Suibhne* or Sweeney Geilt) was the ruler of Dál nAraidi in Ulster, and a warrior king known for his fierce temperament. His life took a tragic turn during the Battle of Mag Rath in the 7th century, when he was cursed with madness and forced to live as a wandering outcast.

The story of his descent into madness is one of the most poignant tales in Irish mythology, blending themes of war, divine punishment, and the delicate relationship between man and nature.

The story begins when Saint Rónán Finn, a Christian holy man, arrived in Sweeney's kingdom and began ringing his bell to announce his presence as he set up a church. This noise greatly irritated Sweeney, who was known for his volatile temper. In a fit of rage, Sweeney rushed to confront the saint, violently grabbing him and throwing his psalter (a book of psalms) into a nearby lake. Saint Rónán, humiliated and angered by Sweeney's disrespect for his religious mission, cursed the king. He foretold that Sweeney would lose his sanity and live out his days wandering in the wild like a bird.

Shortly after this confrontation, Sweeney went to war at the Battle of Mag Rath, fighting alongside the men of Ulster. As the battle raged, Sweeney's curse began to take hold. In the midst of the conflict, the sounds of clashing weapons and the chaos of the battlefield overwhelmed him. His mind, already unstable from the curse, snapped, and he was seized by an uncontrollable urge to flee. Abandoning the battle, Sweeney leapt into the air, his body becoming weightless, as if he had taken on the characteristics of a bird.

From that moment, Sweeney's life was forever changed. He was driven mad, wandering through forests, mountains, and valleys, living like a wild creature. His curse not only affected his mind but also gave him an unnatural ability to leap

across great distances, allowing him to move swiftly through the treetops and over rivers. He survived by eating watercress and drinking from streams, disconnected from the human world he had once ruled.

Though Sweeney's body was still human, his mind was filled with the thoughts and instincts of a bird. He could no longer tolerate human company, and the once-mighty king became a solitary, tragic figure. His only companions were the wild creatures of the forest, and he was consumed by loneliness and sorrow. The transformation was not just physical—Sweeney's madness made him painfully aware of the fragile, fleeting nature of life, and he spent much of his time composing poetic laments for his lost kingdom and former life.

Sweeney's wanderings lasted for many years. During this time, he experienced moments of temporary clarity, but his madness always returned. He became a symbol of the fragility of the human mind, torn between the natural and civilized worlds. In the end, Sweeney's life came to a tragic conclusion. He sought refuge at the house of Saint Moling, where he found temporary peace. However, his violent death came at the hands of a swineherd who stabbed him with a spear, bringing an end to his years of wandering.

Above: A modern interpretation of the madness of king Sweeney, sourced from the Irish blogsite Kingdom Poets, by D.S. Martin: *Sweeney Astray*; **Opposite:** *Suibhne*. Another modern image depicting the mad king, from Irish site *Leabhar Breac*

THE STORY OF NIALL OF THE NINE HOSTAGES

Niall of the Nine Hostages, one of the most legendary High Kings of Ireland, was born into a complex and turbulent family.

Above: Portrait of Niall Noígíallach, sourced from Celtic Native

Niall's father, Eochaid Mugmedón, was the High King of Tara, and his mother was Cairenn Chasdub, a woman of lowly status. Niall's early life was fraught with conflict, especially with his stepmother, Mongfind, and her sons. Mongfind, who favored her own children, especially Brión, sought to prevent Niall from ascending to the throne.

As Niall grew, it became clear that he possessed great potential. His stepmother, however, tried to ensure that her own sons would gain power. In one infamous story, Mongfind deliberately made Niall and his brothers compete for the throne. The challenge involved retrieving weapons from a burning forge, with the quality of the weapons each brother retrieved serving as a measure of his worth.

Niall entered the forge last, but emerged with the finest weapons, a sign of his future greatness. This contest proved his superiority over his brothers, particularly Brión, and cemented his claim to the throne. Yet Mongfind did not give up her efforts to block Niall's rise to power, and the conflict between the brothers continued.

Another key moment in Niall's story occurred when the druid who served the court at Tara took the brothers to a magical well to test their leadership abilities. They encountered a hideous old woman guarding the well, who offered water in exchange for a kiss. Most of Niall's brothers refused, repelled by her appearance, but Niall, showing both bravery and wisdom, kissed her. In return, the old woman transformed into a

Left: Niall Noígiallach, Niall of the Nine Hostages, the High King of Tara who expanded his power base to become High King of Ireland. His story involves taking military control of the nine regions he invaded, and also parts of Scotland, Britain, and even Gaul. It was on one of these foreign raids that Niall captured a young boy who would later become Saint Patrick, Ireland's patron saint. Sourced from Your Irish; **Below:** Saint Patrick and his entourage on their journey to Tara, Niall's home kingdom, to convert the tribe to Christianity in the 5th-century AD. Courtesy North Wind Picture Archives on Alamy.

beautiful maiden, revealing herself to be the Sovereignty of Ireland, the embodiment of kingship. By kissing her, Niall proved himself worthy to rule, and the druid proclaimed that Niall would become the High King of Ireland.

After securing the throne, Niall's reign was marked by expansion and consolidation of power. His name, Niall of the Nine Hostages, came from his practice of taking hostages from the provinces of Ireland and from foreign lands to ensure their loyalty. These hostages were a symbol of his dominance, representing the nine regions he controlled, which included parts of Ireland, Scotland, and Britain. By taking these hostages, Niall ensured the stability and unity of his kingdom through both diplomacy and force.

Niall was also known for his raids across the seas, particularly in Britain and Gaul. His military campaigns abroad helped solidify his power, and his influence extended far beyond the borders of Ireland. According to legend, it was during one of these raids in Britain that he captured a young boy who would later become Saint Patrick, Ireland's patron saint. Though the historical accuracy of this claim is debated, the story links Niall to one of the most important figures in Irish history.

THE BATTLE OF CLONTARF

On Good Friday, April 23, 1014, the Battle of Clontarf was fought on the shores of Dublin Bay, a clash that would change the course of Irish history.

Above: Engraving of Brian Bóruma mac Cennétig, High King of Ireland. The print is dated 1723

At the heart of the conflict was Brian Boru, the High King of Ireland, who sought to end the dominance of the Viking forces in Ireland and their local allies. The battle was not only a struggle for control over the island but also a personal conflict between Brian and his rivals, particularly Máel Mórda, the King of Leinster, and his Viking allies from Dublin.

Years before the battle, Brian Boru had risen to power, uniting much of Ireland under his kingship and challenging the long-standing control of Viking settlers, who had established strongholds in cities like Dublin, Wexford, and Limerick.

Though Brian had defeated many Viking forces, he still faced opposition from some Irish kings, including Máel Mórda, who resented Brian's dominance.

Máel Mórda and the Viking King of Dublin, Sigtrygg Silkbeard, sought to overthrow Brian's rule. They formed an alliance with Viking mercenaries from across the seas, including forces from the Orkneys and the Isle of Man. Knowing that Brian's forces were strong, they planned a decisive battle at Clontarf, a coastal plain near Dublin. Brian Boru, though in his seventies and no longer able to fight himself, led an army consisting of warriors from Munster, Connacht, and other Irish provinces loyal to him. His son, Murchad, commanded the army on the battlefield.

The battle began at dawn, with both sides clashing fiercely. The Viking forces, led by Earl Sigurd of Orkney and Brodir of Man,

fought with their characteristic brutality. Brian's Irish forces, however, were equally determined, spurred on by their king's vision of freeing Ireland from foreign domination. The battlefield stretched along the coast, and as the tide began to rise, the fighting became more intense.

Murchad, Brian's son, fought valiantly at the head of his troops, cutting down many Viking warriors. The Irish gained ground as the day wore on, slowly pushing the Vikings back toward the sea. Many of the Viking forces, unfamiliar with the tidal conditions along the coast, were trapped as the water began to rise, cutting off their retreat. Sigurd and many other Viking leaders were slain in the chaos, and the combined forces of Máel Mórda and the Vikings began to crumble under the relentless pressure of Brian's army.

Despite the Irish victory, the battle came at a great cost. Brian Boru, too old to fight on the battlefield, had remained in his tent, praying for victory. As the battle neared its end, the Viking leader Brodir, seeing the defeat of his forces, made a desperate attempt to salvage his honor. He broke through the Irish lines and found Brian's tent. In a final, brutal act, Brodir entered the tent and killed the High King with a single stroke before being captured and killed himself.

Though Brian Boru died at Clontarf, his forces had won a decisive victory. The power of the Vikings in Ireland was broken, and their influence would never again reach the heights that it had achieved in the past.

Above: Viking leader Brodir steals into Brian Boru's battlefield tent; **Top, main image:** A representation of the Battle of Clontarf on the shores of Dublin Bay, by Hugh Frazer, oil on canvas, 1826

WELSH MYTHOLOGY

2

Welsh mythology is steeped in the ancient beliefs and traditions of Wales and preserved in medieval manuscripts such as the *Mabinogion*. These narratives, marked by themes of transformation, loyalty, and the blurred boundaries between realms, remain a vibrant part of the Celtic mythological tradition and Welsh cultural identity

Opposite: Mountain peaks in Snowdonia, one of the mystical and magical regions of Wales.

MEDIÆVAL WALES
English Miles
0 1 2 3 4 5 10 15 20
+ Ecclesiastical sites
x Sites of Battles
□ Roman sites
REFERENCE TO MAIN DIVISIONS
1 Gwynedd uch Conwy
2 Gwynedd is Conwy
3 Powys Fadog
4 Powys Wenwynwyn
5 Ceredigion
6 Rhwng gwy a Hafren
7 Dyfed
8 Ystrad Tywi
9 Morgannwg
YNYS MÔN
LLIFON
TALYBOLION
TWRCELYN
MALLDRAETH
MENAI
TINDAETHWY
CREUDDYN
RHOS
TEGEINGL
RHUFONIOG
CYMEIRCH
DYFFRYN CLWYD
YSTRAD ALUN
YR HOB
DAL
MAELOR
MAELOR SAESNEG
ARLLECHWEDD
ARFON
NANT CONWY
EIFIONYDD
LLEYN
ARDUDWY
DINMAEL
EDEYRNION
NANHEUDWY
PENLLYN
CYNLLAITH
MOCHNANT
MECHAIN
DEUDDWR
YSTRAD MARCHELL
MAWDDWY
CAEREINION
LLANNERCH HUDOL
MEIRIONYDD
CYFEILIOG
CYDEWAIN
ARWYSTLI
CERI
GENEU'R GLYN
PERFEDD
CREUDDYN
MEFENYDD
ANHUNIOG
PENNARDD
CWMWD DEUDDWR
GWERTHRYNION
MAELIENYDD
BUELLT
LLWYTHYFNWG
ELFAEL
CAERWEDROS
MABWNION
ISCOED
GWINIONYDD
CANTREF MAWR
CANTREF BYCHAN
EMLYN
CEMAIS
PEBIDIOG
DEUGLEDDYF
CANTREF GWARTHAF
RHOS
PENFRO
CYDWELI
CARNWYLLION
GOWER
BRYCHEINIOG
YSTRAD YW
EWIAS LACY
ERGING
GWENT
NEATH
AFAN
TIR YR IARLL
GLYN OGWR
GLYN RHONDDA
MEISGYN
SENGHENYDD
GWYNLLWG
COETY

INTRODUCTION

Deeply rooted in their Celtic past, the stories of Wales have been passed down through countless generations, often blending myth, folklore, and early history.

***The Mabinogion*, a collection of medieval Welsh tales, forms the core of Welsh mythology, recounting stories of gods, heroes, enchantresses, and otherworldly beings.**

The tales encompass themes of magic, transformation, loyalty, and the relationship between the natural and supernatural realms, preserving the essence and mythic heritage of Wales.

The Four Branches of *The Mabinogion*

The Mabinogion is the most well-known source of Welsh mythology, comprising eleven stories, four of which are collectively known as the Four Branches of the Mabinogi. Each branch focuses on different characters and events, but they are all interconnected, creating a cohesive narrative that reflects the mythology of early Wales.

The First Branch follows Pwyll, Prince of Dyfed, and his adventures in the otherworld, his encounter with Arawn, and his marriage to Rhiannon. The Second Branch tells of Branwen, daughter of Llŷr. The Third Branch centers on Manawydan, the son of Llŷr, and his trials following the devastation brought upon his family. The Fourth Branch introduces Math, son of Mathonwy, and his complex relationship with his nephews Gwydion and Gilfaethwy, as well as the tragic fate of Lleu Llaw Gyffes.

Themes and the Supernatural

Welsh mythology is characterized by its deep connection to the natural world and the supernatural. The otherworld, known as *Annwn*, plays a significant role in many of the stories. Annwn is portrayed as a parallel realm, often depicted as a place of beauty, abundance, and magic, but also one that can be dangerous and unpredictable. The interaction between the mortal world and Annwn is a recurring theme, with heroes often journeying into the otherworld to fulfill quests, face trials, or gain wisdom.

Transformation is another prominent theme in Welsh mythology, with many characters undergoing physical or spiritual changes. The story of Taliesin, who transforms multiple times to escape Ceridwen, and the tale of Blodeuwedd, a woman created from flowers and later transformed into an owl, are just two examples of how transformation is used to explore identity and fate.

The magical landscape of Wales itself plays an essential role in shaping the mythology. The mountains, lakes, and forests of Wales are more than just settings—they are integral to the stories, often acting as thresholds between the human world and the realms of gods, spirits, and other supernatural beings.

Above: *The Mabinogion*, the British Penguin Classics edition from 1977, translated by Jeffrey Gantz. The front cover shows a detail from *The Four Queens* by David Jones, in Tate Britain, London; **Opposite:** A medieval map of the regions of Wales, from *A History of Wales from the Earliest Times to the Edwardian Conquest*, published 1911, by John Edward Lloyd. These regions would in Celtic times have, more or less, represented the old kingdoms. They're all numbered, and the Key, top left, shows: 1) *Gwynedd uch Conwy*; 2) *Gwynedd is Conwy*; 3) *Powys Fadog*; 4) *Powys Wenwynwyn*; 5) *Ceredigion*; 6) *Rhwng gwy a Hafren*; 7) *Dyfed*; 8) *Ystrad Tywi*; 9) *Morgannwg*. Map by George Philip & Son Ltd for The London Geographical Institute.

MYTHOLOGICAL FAMILIES

Welsh mythology is full of stories of gods, heroes, and legendary figures, many of whom belong to interconnected mythological families.

These mythological families form the backbone of the *Mabinogion*. Central to Welsh mythology are the family dynamics, conflicts, and relationships that shape the actions and fates of these powerful figures. The most significant mythological families are those of Dôn, Llŷr, and Pwyll, each representing different aspects of Welsh mythology, including nature, magic, and the connection between the mortal and otherworldly realms.

The Family of Dôn

The family of Dôn, known as *the Children of Dôn*, is one of the most prominent mythological lineages in Welsh mythology. Dôn herself is often depicted as a mother goddess, and her descendants are powerful figures connected to the forces of nature, magic, and sovereignty.

The Children of Dôn play a major role in the Fourth Branch of the *Mabinogion*, where they are involved in conflicts with rival families and undergo trials that test their strength and ingenuity.

Among the most notable members of this family are Gwydion, a master magician and trickster, and Arianrhod, a goddess of the moon and fertility. Gwydion's cunning and magical abilities are central to several stories, including the creation of Blodeuwedd, a woman made of flowers, as a bride for his nephew Lleu Llaw Gyffes.

Arianrhod, who is Gwydion's sister, is a complex figure whose actions significantly shape the fate of Lleu. The Children of Dôn are often associated with magic, transformation, and the challenges of family loyalty, as their stories explore themes of betrayal, resilience, and the use of power.

The Family of Llŷr

The family of Llŷr, known as *the Children of Llŷr*, represents another key lineage in Welsh mythology, often associated with the sea and the forces of nature. Llŷr himself is a god of the sea, and his children play important roles in the myths that illustrate the balance between order and chaos.

The most significant members of this family are Bran the Blessed (Bendigeidfran), Branwen, and Manawydan. Bran the Blessed is a giant, and also a powerful king, known for his wisdom and strength. He plays a central role in the Second Branch of the *Mabinogion*, which tells the story of Branwen's ill-fated marriage to the Irish king Matholwch. The tale of Branwen's mistreatment and the ensuing war between the Britons and the Irish reveals the tragic consequences of familial loyalty and betrayal.

Bran's death, and the preservation of his head as a talisman to protect Britain, speaks to his enduring connection to the land and his role as a protector of his people.

Manawydan, Bran's brother, is another significant figure in Welsh mythology. He appears in the Third Branch of the *Mabinogion*, where he marries Rhiannon, a figure associated with magic and sovereignty. Together, they face numerous challenges, including enchantments and trials that threaten their livelihood. The stories of the Children of Llŷr often revolve around themes of loss, resilience, and the interplay between the human and otherworldly realms.

The Family of Pwyll and Rhiannon

The family of Pwyll, ruler of Dyfed, and Rhiannon, a goddess-like figure, is also central to Welsh mythology. Their story is told in the First and Third Branches of the *Mabinogion*. Pwyll, through a series of adventures, wins the love of Rhiannon, and they marry, forming a union that brings together the mortal and divine realms.

Their son, Pryderi, is one of the few figures who appears in all four branches of the *Mabinogion*, serving as a link between different stories and characters. His abduction as an infant and his eventual return, as well as his adventures as an adult, illustrate themes of loss, restoration, and the complexities of fate.

The family of Pwyll and Rhiannon is often associated with the interplay between the natural and supernatural, and their tales explore the trials and tribulations of kingship, marriage, and parenthood in a world where the boundaries between reality and magic are fluid.

Opposite: The majestic peaks of Cadair Idris, Snowdonia, in winter. *Idris* is usually taken to be the name of a giant or, alternatively, it may refer to *Idris ap Gwyddno*, a 7th-century prince of Meirionnydd who fought and won a battle against the Irish on the mountain.

THE *MABIN*

The *Mabinogion* is one of the most important collections of Welsh tales, preserving the myths, legends, and folklore of ancient Wales.

Above: The front cover of a deluxe version of the *Mabinogion*, as translated by Lady Charlotte Guest in the years 1838–45, then published bilingually in English and Welsh. This edition features the work of renowned British illustrator Alan Lee, who was later to be instrumental in the visual concept and set designs of Peter Jackson's *The Lord of the Rings* movies; **Above right:** *Dwyn pen Bendigeidfran i Lundain,* an early 20th-century pen and ink book illustration by Thomas Heath Robinson, depicting the ceremony of returning home the head of Bran the Blessed to Britain, after he was mortally wounded in the battle with Matholwch, the King of Ireland (see pages 142–143)

Comprising eleven stories, these tales span a variety of genres, blending history, mythology, folklore—and the early roots of Arthurian romance. The *Mabinogion* holds a key place in Welsh cultural heritage, offering a window into the Celtic worldview, the values of a medieval, and pre-medieval, Welsh society, and the long, enduring customs that have shaped a national identity.

ORIGIN AND MANUSCRIPTS

Its stories are descended, and have evolved from, the ancient oral storytelling tradition of Celtic Wales—that is, from the Britain of around 600 BC (though the Celtic language itself dates back much further).

Perhaps some *fifteen hundred to two thousand years later*, they were compiled by Christian scribes into a contemporary written form in two major manuscripts: *The White Book of Rhydderch*, circa 1350, and *The Red Book of Hergest*, circa 1400. These manuscripts are essential sources

OGION

of early Welsh literature, containing the oldest-known versions of these ancient and lasting tales.

The name "Mabinogion" is derived from the word "mab," meaning "boy" or "son," but its exact meaning is debated among scholars. The term was popularized by Lady Charlotte Guest, who translated the tales into English in the 19th century. She mistakenly used "Mabinogion" as the title for the entire collection, and it has since become the accepted name for these stories.

STRUCTURE AND CONTENT

The *Mabinogion*'s eleven tales can be divided into different groups, based on their themes and origins. The core of the collection is formed by the Four Branches of the Mabinogi—*Pwyll, Prince of Dyfed*; *Branwen, Daughter of Llŷr*; *Manawydan, Son of Llŷr*; and *Math, Son of Mathonwy*. These four stories are interconnected and feature recurring characters, exploring themes of sovereignty, magic, and the relationships between the human and otherworldly realms. The Four Branches form a cohesive narrative that reflects the complexities of Welsh mythology and the interplay between the natural and supernatural worlds.

In addition to the Four Branches, the Mabinogion also includes three independent romances—*Owain, or the Lady of the Fountain*; *Peredur, Son of Efrawg*; and *Geraint and Enid*. These stories have strong ties to Arthurian legend and show the influence of Continental romance literature, blending traditional Welsh elements with chivalric ideals. The romances depict the adventures of knights associated with King Arthur's court, incorporating themes of love, honor, and the quest for identity.

The collection also features other tales of myth and folklore, such as *Culhwch and Olwen*, one of the earliest Arthurian tales, in which the hero Culhwch seeks the help of Arthur and his warriors to win the hand of Olwen. *The Dream of Macsen Wledig* tells the semi-mythical story of the Roman Emperor Magnus Maximus, while *The Dream of Rhonabwy* is a visionary tale involving Arthur and his warriors. *The Tale of Lludd and Llefelys* recounts the adventures of two brothers, dealing with threats to the kingdom of Britain.

THEMES AND SYMBOLISM

The Mabinogion is rich with themes that reflect the values and beliefs of medieval Welsh society. The interplay between the natural and supernatural worlds is a recurring motif, with many of the characters having direct contact with otherworldly beings or places.

The stories explore the themes of kingship, honor, loyalty, and the complex relationships between individuals, communities, and the divine. They also emphasize the importance of fate and destiny, with many characters undergoing trials that reveal their true nature and roles within the larger cosmic order.

The Arthurian tales within the Mabinogion are notable for their distinctly Welsh perspective, portraying Arthur as a hero and leader who embodies the values of strength, justice, and generosity. Unlike the later English and Continental portrayals of Arthur as a romanticized, tragic figure, the Arthur of the *Mabinogion* is a dynamic and formidable leader whose adventures are interwoven with the fate of Britain.

Top: *Drudwy Branwen*, Branwen's Starling, Margaret Jones, watercolor, to illustrate Gwyn Thomas's *Tales from the Mabinogion*. Courtesy People's Collection Wales; **Above**: Llud and Llefelys: The Battle of the Dragons, drawn 1881 by Alfred Fredericks, from *Knightly Legends of Wales or The Boy's Mabinogion, Being the Earliest Welsh Tales of King Arthur in the Famous Red Book of Hergest*, by Mary D. Lanier

THE WELSH DRAGON

The Welsh Dragon, known as *Y Ddraig Goch*, is one of the most iconic symbols of Welsh mythology and national identity.

Above: A Welsh dragon in Cardiff; **Top:** Welsh dragon stained glass window in St. Gwyddelan's Church, Dolwyddelan, Gwynedd

Depicted as a powerful red dragon, it features prominently in the national flag of Wales and is often associated with the resilience, strength, and cultural pride of the Welsh people.

The origin of the Welsh Dragon is deeply rooted in myth, with ties to both the ancient Celtic tradition and later medieval literature, reflecting the unique history and identity of Wales.

MYTHOLOGICAL ORIGINS

The Welsh Dragon's earliest origins can be traced to Celtic mythology, where dragons were seen as protectors of the earth and guardians of sacred places. The red dragon of Wales is often linked to the stories of the Britons, the Celtic inhabitants of Britain, and is closely tied to the lore of the early British kings. The dragon is believed to symbolize the fierce spirit of the Welsh people, representing both their connection to the land and their enduring struggle against various invaders over the centuries.

One of the most well-known myths involving the Welsh Dragon is recorded in Geoffrey of Monmouth's *Historia Regum Britanniae* (*The History of the Kings of Britain*), written in the 12th century. In this tale, the young Merlin—known as *Myrddin* in Welsh—reveals the story of two battling dragons, one red and one white, beneath the foundations of King Vortigern's fortress. Vortigern, a ruler in early Britain, had attempted to build his stronghold on a hill, but each night, the foundations collapsed. Merlin was summoned, and he

revealed that the instability was caused by two dragons fighting beneath the earth. The red dragon represented the native Britons, while the white dragon symbolized the invading Saxons. In Merlin's prophecy, the red dragon's eventual victory foretold the triumph of the Britons over their enemies, becoming a powerful symbol of Welsh resistance and hope (See also pages 190–191).

SYMBOLISM AND EVOLUTION

The Welsh Dragon holds significant symbolism in Welsh culture. The red color of the dragon represents both the fiery nature of the creature and the resilience of the Welsh people. Its association with protection and the guardianship of the land resonates with the historical struggles of the Welsh, who faced numerous invasions and attempts to suppress their culture.

Over time, the Welsh Dragon became more than just a mythological creature; it evolved into a symbol of national identity. During the medieval period, it was adopted by various Welsh rulers, including Cadwaladr, a 7th-century king of Gwynedd. Cadwaladr's association with the red dragon further solidified its status as an emblem of Welsh royalty and resistance. The image of the red dragon was also popularized during the Welsh rebellions against English rule, reinforcing its role as a symbol of defiance and the fight for independence.

The Welsh Dragon's significance grew during the reign of the Tudor dynasty, which had Welsh origins. Henry VII, who was of Welsh descent, used the red dragon as part of his royal standard when he defeated Richard III at the Battle of Bosworth in 1485. This helped elevate the dragon as a symbol of both royal power and the proud heritage of the Welsh people.

Above: The Welsh Dragon sculpture which surmounts the dome of Cardiff City Hall in Cathays Park, Cardiff, by Henry Charles Fehr; **Top:** The red dragon, the key element of the national flag of Wales

PWYLL, PRINCE OF DYFED

Pwyll, Prince of Dyfed, was a lord known for his honor and sense of adventure. His tale begins when he set out on a hunting trip in the mystical land of Dyfed, a region renowned for its deep forests and hidden magic.

Top: *Pwyll, Prince of Dyfed*, watercolour, by renowned British illustrator Alan Lee; **Above:** *Arawn, the ruler of the Otherworld*, by Avid Archer

During his hunt, Pwyll became separated from his companions and ventured deeper into the woods, where he came across a pack of strange, ethereal hounds. Unlike his own hounds, these were white with red ears, and they were surrounding a stag.

Recognizing their supernatural nature, Pwyll nevertheless chased the hounds away and claimed the stag for himself. Shortly after, a mysterious figure appeared, a man of regal bearing and an otherworldly presence. He introduced himself as Arawn, the ruler of *Annwn*, the mystical Otherworld. Arawn was displeased with Pwyll's actions, for Pwyll had unknowingly interfered with a hunt sacred to *Annwn*.

To atone for this transgression, Arawn proposed a unique arrangement: the two men would switch places for a year and a day. Pwyll would rule *Annwn* in Arawn's stead, and in return, he would face Arawn's greatest enemy, Hafgan, a rival king, in single combat.

Pwyll, eager to make amends, agreed to Arawn's conditions. Arawn used his magic to transform Pwyll into his exact likeness, while Arawn took on Pwyll's form to rule Dyfed. During the year in *Annwn*, Pwyll lived as Arawn, experiencing the wonders of the Otherworld. He ruled with wisdom and restraint, ensuring that none suspected the switch. When the day of the duel

arrived, Pwyll faced Hafgan and, with a single blow, defeated him, sparing his life as Arawn had advised. This act not only ended the conflict but also solidified Arawn's power over *Annwn*.

Throughout the year, Pwyll showed great loyalty to Arawn, even refusing to approach Arawn's queen, maintaining her honor as if she were his own wife. When the year ended, Arawn and Pwyll resumed their true forms, and Arawn was deeply grateful for Pwyll's loyalty, wisdom, and success. They parted as lifelong friends, with Arawn declaring Pwyll the honorary title *Pwyll Pen Annwn*, meaning "Pwyll, Head of Annwn," in recognition of his deeds.

Upon his return to Dyfed, Pwyll found that Arawn had ruled his land well, and Pwyll's people were content and thriving. Pwyll, having learned much from his time in Annwn, continued to rule with even greater wisdom and fairness.

Later, Pwyll encountered a mysterious woman named Rhiannon, who rode a white

horse at a pace that seemed uncatchable, even when pursued at full speed. Struck by her beauty and intrigued by her magic, Pwyll called out to her, and she willingly stopped. Rhiannon revealed that she had chosen Pwyll as her suitor, rejecting another, more undesirable match. Pwyll, captivated by her grace and determination, agreed to marry her, setting in motion a series of adventures that would shape the rest of his life and bring both joy and sorrow to his kingdom.

BRANWEN, DAUGHTER OF LLŶR

Branwen, the daughter of Llŷr and sister to *Bendigeidfran*—Bran the Blessed, the giant King of Britain—was known throughout the kingdom for her beauty and nobility.

Above left: Matholwch, the King of Ireland. Courtesy of Roman-Britain.co.uk; **Above right:** *Branwen*, by Christopher Williams. First exhibited at the Royal Academy in 1915 and now in the Collection of the Glynn Vivian Art Gallery, City of Swansea; **Opposite, main image:** Bran the Blessed, the giant King of Britain, arrives in Ireland with his mighty force, determined to rescue his sister Branwen and restore her honor. Courtesy of Roman-Britain.co.uk; **Opposite, below:** *Procession of the Blessed Head* by Peter Diamond. Bran the Blessed is mortally wounded in the battle with Matholwch's army by a poisoned spear to his foot, and he commands his men to cut off his head and take it back to Britain. Diamond's illustration depicts the taking of his head to *Gwynfryn*, the White Hill—believed to be the site of the White Tower, subsequently the earliest building of the Tower of London. Buried there, it guarded Britain from foreign invasion, until its later excavation during the rule of King Arthur.

Her story begins when Matholwch, the High King of Ireland, arrived in Wales seeking an alliance with Bran's people. Matholwch sought the hand of Branwen in marriage as a gesture of goodwill between their kingdoms. Bran the Blessed, the giant King of Britain, welcomed Matholwch warmly, and after consulting with his advisors, he agreed to the marriage proposal.

A grand feast was held, and Branwen and Matholwch were married, creating a union that promised peace between Wales and Ireland. However, not all were pleased with this alliance. Efnysien, Branwen's half-brother, was enraged that he had not been consulted about the marriage. In a fit of anger and jealousy, Efnysien mutilated Matholwch's prized horses, cutting off their ears, lips, and tails. This act of cruelty deeply insulted Matholwch and threatened to unravel the fragile peace between the two kingdoms.

To prevent hostilities, Bran offered Matholwch compensation, including gifts of gold, horses, and a magical cauldron that could restore the dead to life, although the revived would be unable to speak. Despite his initial outrage, Matholwch accepted the reparations, and he and Branwen returned to Ireland, where they hoped to begin their life together in peace.

However, when they returned to Ireland, the wounds of Efnysien's insult festered among the Irish people. Soon, whispers of resentment grew into acts of cruelty against Branwen.

Matholwch, bowing to the pressure of his lords, allowed Branwen to be mistreated. She was stripped of her royal status and forced to work in the kitchens, enduring harsh treatment daily. Despite her suffering, Branwen remained resilient. During her time in captivity, she befriended a starling, which she trained to carry a message across the sea to her brother Bran.

The starling, loyal and swift, flew across the Irish Sea to Wales, finding Bran the Blessed and delivering Branwen's message of distress. Upon learning of his sister's plight, Bran was filled with anger and sorrow. He immediately gathered his forces and crossed the sea to Ireland, determined to rescue his beloved sister and restore her honor. Bran's arrival in Ireland with a massive army led to a tense confrontation.

Matholwch, fearful of the great giant and his forces, initially sought to make peace. However, mistrust ran deep, and despite efforts to negotiate, violence erupted. A brutal battle ensued, known as the Second Branch of the Mabinogi.

During the fighting, Efnysien, realizing the harm he had caused, sacrificed himself to destroy Matholwch's forces and the magical cauldron used to revive the dead. The battle left countless dead on both sides, and even Bran himself was mortally wounded. As he lay dying, Bran instructed his men to cut off his head and take it back to

Britain, where it would continue to provide protection to the Kingdom.

Branwen was able to return to Wales, but her heart was broken. Overwhelmed by the catastrophic war between Britain and Ireland, and the loss of her son, her husband, and three of her brothers, she blamed herself for the tragedy and could not bear the sorrow. Soon after, she died of grief, and her body was buried on the banks of the *Afon Alaw*, the River Alaw, on the Isle of Anglesey, off the coast of North Wales.

MANAWYDAN, SON OF LLŶR

Manawydan, the son of Llŷr and brother of Bran the Blessed, was known for his wisdom and steadiness, traits that would serve him well through times of trial. After the tragic events in Ireland, which led to the deaths of Bran and many of their kin, Manawydan returned to Wales with the survivors, including Pryderi, the son of Pwyll, and Rhiannon, Pryderi's mother.

Above: Rhiannon finds Pryderi, entrapped at the magical cauldron, drawn 1881 by Alfred Fredericks from *Knightly Legends of Wales or The Boy's Mabinogion, Being the Earliest Welsh Tales of King Arthur in the Famous Red Book of Hergest*, by Mary D. Lanier, New York, copyright 1909 and 1912.

Manawydan was welcomed by Branwen's people, but with the loss of his brother and the disintegration of his family's power, he felt as if he had no real place in the land that was once his own.

Seeing his grief and longing for stability, Pryderi offered Manawydan his mother's hand in marriage. Rhiannon, a figure of great grace and mystery, had suffered her own share of sorrows, and she agreed to marry Manawydan, finding solace in his wisdom and kindness. Together with Pryderi and Pryderi's wife, Cigfa, the four settled in Dyfed, hoping for a peaceful life.

For a time, they lived happily, but one day, as they were out hunting, a strange mist descended upon the land of Dyfed. When the mist cleared, the once-thriving kingdom had become barren and desolate. The people, livestock, and vitality of the land had vanished, leaving only Manawydan, Rhiannon, Pryderi, and Cigfa in a silent, empty world.

Faced with this eerie curse, the group left Dyfed to try and make a living elsewhere. They traveled east into England, where Manawydan and Pryderi put their skills to use as craftsmen. Manawydan, who was particularly skilled in leatherwork and saddle-making, earned a reputation for his high-quality craftsmanship. However, the locals, jealous of their skill and unable to compete, drove them away. Manawydan and his companions moved from place to place, but each time, their success led to jealousy and hostility, forcing them to leave.

Eventually, they returned to the barren land of Dyfed. One day, Pryderi and Manawydan were hunting when they discovered a mysterious shimmering boar. The boar led them to a deserted castle, and Pryderi, unable to resist its strange attraction, entered, and found himself magnetized to a magical cauldron. Manawydan, recognizing the danger, tried to save Pryderi but was unable. Pryderi was trapped by the magic, and Manawydan had no choice but to

return home alone to Rhiannon and Cigfa. Soon after, Rhiannon herself, searching for her son, also fell victim to the castle's enchantment, leaving only Manawydan and Cigfa. Despite his grief, Manawydan remained determined to save his loved ones. He began to devise a plan to break the curse that had befallen Dyfed.

He cultivated the land, but was dismayed to see that the field he had planted the previous day was laid waste. He set a trap, capturing a mouse that had eaten the grain. The mouse, however, was no ordinary creature, but the enchanted wife of Llwyd ap Cil Coed, who had cast the curse on Dyfed in retaliation for the harm done to his friend Gwawl by Pwyll, Pryderi's father.

Manawydan threatened to hang the mouse, and soon, a series of mysterious figures appeared, offering him rewards to let it go. Manawydan, however, refused each offer until Llwyd himself appeared, pleading for the release of his wife. Manawydan demanded that the curse be lifted, and that Pryderi and Rhiannon be freed from their enchantment. Llwyd agreed, and with his magic, restored Dyfed and released Manawydan's family.

With the return of the people and the land's prosperity, Manawydan, Rhiannon, Pryderi, and Cigfa were able to live in peace once more. Manawydan's patience, intelligence, and refusal to succumb to despair had broken the curse, restoring not only his loved ones but also the kingdom of Dyfed.

Top: Pryderi and Manawydan encounter the shimmering boar, which leads them onto the enchanted castle. Courtesy of Roman-Britain.co.uk; **Right:** As Manawydan prepares to kill the mouse who had been eating all his planted grains, Llwyd ap Cil Coed appears, pleading for the release of his enchanted wife who had taken the form of the mouse. Manawydan demands the curse upon Dyfed be lifted, and Rhiannon and Pryderi be released from their enchanted state at the castle. Illustrated by Thomas Heath Robinson, circa early-20th-century. Robinson was the elder brother of the more well-known Heath Robinson.

Math, the son of Mathonwy, was a king of Gwynedd who possessed extraordinary magical abilities, but he had one peculiar need...he could only find comfort if his feet were rubbed and soothed in the lap of a virgin...

Top: King Math is pleasured by his virgin foot-holder Goewin. A Modern Fantasy AI-generated illustration, courtesy of roman-britain.co.uk; **Right:** "A wife for Lleu was made out of flowers." *Blodeuwedd; Flower Face* by Christopher Williams, 1930. Oil on canvas. Collection of the Newport Museum and Art Gallery, Newport, Wales; **Opposite:** Punishment for Gwydion and Gilfaethwy—transformed into deer, wild boar, then wolves, and each year swapping sex, forced to mate and bear offspring...

MATH, SON OF METHONWY

King Math's foot-holder at the time was Goewin, a maiden of great beauty and purity. Math's nephews, Gwydion and Gilfaethwy, served him loyally, but Gilfaethwy secretly harbored a deep desire for Goewin.

Gwydion, ever the schemer and master of magic, devised a plan to fulfill his brother's desire. He suggested to Math that they provoke a war with Pryderi, the ruler of Dyfed, so that Math would have to leave his court, allowing Gilfaethwy to act on his desires. Gwydion stole Pryderi's prized pigs, gifts from the Otherworld, knowing that this would provoke a conflict. He used his magic to transform his men into different shapes, deceiving Pryderi, who declared war in response.

Math, forced to take up arms, left his court, leaving Goewin unprotected. Gilfaethwy took advantage of the situation, sexually assaulting Goewin while Math was away. The war with Pryderi ensued, and through Gwydion's cunning, they managed to defeat Pryderi. Gwydion himself fought Pryderi in single combat, and Pryderi fell in battle, leaving Gwydion victorious.

Upon returning to his court, Math learned of the terrible crime against Goewin. Outraged by the betrayal of his own nephews, Math took swift action. To make amends, he married Goewin, restoring her honor and elevating her to the status of queen. As punishment for Gwydion and Gilfaethwy, Math used his magical powers to transform them into various pairs of animals over three years: first into deer, then wild boars, and finally wolves.

Each year, they were transformed into opposite sexes, forced to mate and bear offspring. At the end of the three years, Math forgave them and restored them to human form, but the experience had humbled them.

With Goewin now married to Math, a new virgin foot-holder was required. Math turned to Arianrhod, his niece, to take on this role. To prove her purity, Arianrhod had to undergo a magical test: stepping over Math's wand. However, to everyone's surprise, as she stepped over the wand, she immediately gave birth to two children. The first was Dylan, who took to the sea and swam away, while the second, an unformed lump, was taken by Gwydion, who nurtured and shaped it into a boy named Lleu Llaw Gyffes.

Arianrhod, humiliated by this revelation, refused to acknowledge Lleu as her son and placed several curses upon him, denying him a name, arms, and a wife. Gwydion, ever resourceful, used his magic to overcome each of these curses. He tricked Arianrhod into giving Lleu a name and arms, and later helped Math create a wife for Lleu out of flowers. They named her Blodeuwedd, meaning "flower face."

LLUD AND LLEFELYS

Llud and Llefelys were two brothers, both noble rulers, whose close bonds and wisdom would be tested by three challenges that threatened the stability of Llud's kingdom.

Llud Llaw Eraint (Llud of the Silver Hand) ruled over Britain, while his younger brother Llefelys was given the kingdom of Gaul. The two were close and frequently communicated, even after Llefelys married a princess of Gaul and established his rule there.

During Llud's reign, a sequence of mysterious plagues fell upon Britain, causing great suffering among the people. These plagues seemed to have no natural explanation, leading Llud to seek advice from his wise and resourceful brother.

The first plague was the arrival of the Coraniaid, a powerful race of dwarfish invaders whose magical abilities made them impossible to defeat. They were said to be able to hear every sound and whisper across the land, making it impossible to plan any attack against them.

The second plague was an eerie, nightly scream that terrified the entire kingdom, robbing the people of their rest and health. This agonizing sound filled the air each night, causing unease and leaving the kingdom in disarray. The third plague was more subtle but equally damaging: every feast held in Llud's court would see all the food and drink mysteriously vanish before anyone could partake.

In his distress, Llud traveled to Gaul to seek the advice of Llefelys. To avoid the prying ears of the Coraniaid, Llefelys devised a clever plan. He used a brass horn to communicate with Llud, so their words would not be heard by the invaders. After listening to the details of the plagues, Llefelys offered his brother advice on how to address each one.

To defeat the Coraniaid, Llefelys explained that they could be destroyed by a concoction made from crushed insects. The insects were harmless to all except the Coraniaid. Llud gathered the insects and prepared the potion as instructed. He then called all the people of Britain together, and under the guise of a grand festival, he spread the concoction across the gathering. The Coraniaid, who were present, were killed, freeing the land from their oppression.

The second plague, the nightly scream, was revealed to be caused by two warring dragons that fought in Britain. One

dragon was native, symbolizing the people of Britain, while the other was foreign, representing the invaders.

Llefelys instructed Llud to find the exact center of Britain, where he should dig a pit and fill it with mead. Following these instructions, Llud did as his brother advised. The dragons, lured by the sweet scent, drank the mead and fell asleep, allowing Llud to capture and bury them in a stone chest beneath Dinas Emrys, his ancient fortress and stronghold. Thus ended the nightly screams.

The third plague, the vanishing feast, was caused by a powerful magician who used his skills to steal from Llud's court. Llefelys advised his brother to prepare a great feast and to stand guard over it himself, keeping a watchful eye. Llud did as he was told and eventually came face to face with the magician. After a fierce struggle, Llud overcame the intruder, ending the final plague. With the help of his brother Llefelys, Llud was able to rid Britain of the three plagues, and peace and stability was restored once more to the kingdom.

Above: Llud listens intently to his brother Llefelys, who counsels him on the courses of action necessary to rid the kingdom of the three plagues that have infected his lands. A Modern Fantasy AI-generated illustration, courtesy of roman-britain.co.uk; **Right:** The Battle of the Dragons, drawn 1881 by Alfred Fredericks from *Knightly Legends of Wales or The Boy's Mabinogion, Being the Earliest Welsh Tales of King Arthur in the Famous Red Book of Hergest*, by Mary D. Lanier, New York, copyright 1909 and 1912.

CULHWCH AND OLWEN

Above: Culhwch, with his greyhounds, arrives at Arthur's court, to be greeted by Glewlwyd Gavaelvawr, Arthur's porter, who initially denies him entry to the palace; **Top:** A Modern Fantasy AI-generated illustration of the early Welsh version of Culhwch's cousin, King Arthur, and his court. Courtesy of roman-britain.co.uk

Culhwch, the son of Cilydd, was cursed by his stepmother, who declared that if Culhwch would not marry her daughter, then he would never marry anyone... except Olwen, the daughter of the fearsome giant chieftain Ysbaddaden Bencawr.

However, Culhwch had heard tell of the grace and beauty of the giant's daughter, and was determined to marry her anyway. Knowing he would need powerful allies to succeed in his quest, he set out for the court of his cousin, King Arthur.

Upon reaching Arthur's court, Culhwch made a bold request for help, invoking their family bond. Arthur agreed and summoned his best warriors, including Kai, Bedwyr, and Gwrhyr, to accompany Culhwch on his quest.

Their journey took them to Ysbaddaden's fortress, hidden in a rugged, wild land. They managed to gain entry and present Culhwch's demand to marry Olwen. Ysbaddaden, whose death had been prophesied on the occasion of his daughter's marriage, was not about to let her go easily. He gave Culhwch a series of almost impossible tasks, called *anoethau*, designed to deter him. There were forty tasks in all, each as daunting as the next.

Among the challenges were capturing the

fearsome boar Twrch Trwyth, retrieving the blood of the Black Witch, and obtaining the cauldron of Diwrnach.

Twrch Trwyth, a monstrous boar, was said to carry a comb, shears, and a razor between its ears, and hunting it was a perilous undertaking. Ysbaddaden was convinced that Culhwch would fail and never return to claim Olwen.

With the support of Arthur and his warriors, Culhwch set out to fulfill these tasks. They traveled across the land, facing fierce enemies and confronting powerful magic. Kai, known for his extraordinary abilities, and Bedwyr, renowned for his skill in battle, were instrumental in overcoming the challenges before them. Together, they retrieved the magical items, confronted sorcerers, and hunted the monstrous boar.

After much hardship, Culhwch and his companions succeeded in fulfilling all of Ysbaddaden's demands. Each time they completed a task, they returned to the giant's fortress, and Ysbaddaden grew more fearful, knowing that his fate was drawing near. With every task fulfilled, the prophecy edged closer to completion.

When the final task was completed, Ysbaddaden could no longer prevent the marriage. On the day of the wedding, the giant met his end, slain by Culhwch and his companions, as was foretold. With Ysbaddaden's death, Culhwch was finally able to marry Olwen, and they were united in a grand celebration.

Culhwch's quest for Olwen, aided by Arthur and his loyal knights, marked the end of Ysbaddaden's tyranny and the beginning of a new chapter for the young couple.

Above: Arthur's knights in action during the chase of the fearsome great boar, Twrch Trwyth. Another wonderful watercolor by Alan Lee.

Above: *Ceridwen*, by Christopher Williams, 1910. Collection of the Glynn Vivian Art Gallery, Swansea

THE TALE OF TALIESIN

The story of Taliesin, the great bard and seer, begins with Ceridwen, a powerful enchantress who lived with her husband Tegid Foel and their children, by *Llyn Tegid* (Bala Lake), in Gwynedd.

Ceridwen had a son named Morfran, whose appearance was unfortunate—he was so unattractive that his mother feared he would be rejected by everyone. To compensate for Morfran's lack of physical beauty, Ceridwen decided to brew a potion that would grant him unmatched wisdom and poetic inspiration.

This potion was no ordinary concoction; it needed to be brewed for a year and a day, and only the first three drops were powerful enough to impart wisdom. The rest of the brew was poisonous. Ceridwen enlisted the help of a blind man named Morda to tend the fire, and a young servant boy named Gwion Bach to stir the cauldron.

For a year and a day, Gwion tended the cauldron, watching over the potion as it bubbled and boiled. On the final day, three drops of the scalding liquid splashed onto Gwion's thumb. Without thinking, he put his thumb in his mouth to cool it and immediately felt the rush of the potion's power. With those three drops, Gwion gained insight and foresight, understanding both his fate and Ceridwen's rage at his unintended theft.

Knowing that Ceridwen would not forgive him, Gwion fled. As soon as Ceridwen discovered what had happened, she was furious and set out in pursuit. Using his newfound powers, Gwion transformed himself into a hare to escape, but Ceridwen turned herself into a greyhound, gaining on him swiftly. Gwion then leapt into a river and transformed into a fish, but Ceridwen became an otter, continuing the chase. When Gwion changed into a bird and flew into the sky, Ceridwen followed as a hawk, relentless in her pursuit.

Finally, in desperation, Gwion transformed into a single grain of wheat, hiding among a pile of grain. Ceridwen, however, transformed into a hen and pecked through the pile until she found and swallowed him. But that was not the end—Ceridwen soon discovered that she was pregnant. She knew the child she carried was Gwion reborn, but when he was born, he was so beautiful that she could not bring herself to kill him.

Instead, she placed the infant in a leather bag and set him adrift in the sea. The baby floated until he was found by Elffin, the son of Gwyddno Garanhir. Elffin was a fisherman and a nobleman, and when he opened the bag, he saw the radiant child. The baby, already wise beyond his years, spoke and told Elffin that his name was Taliesin, meaning "radiant brow." Elffin took the child home, raising him as his own.

Taliesin grew into a prodigy, possessing unmatched wisdom and the gift of prophecy. He became a renowned bard, using his talents to aid Elffin and others in need. Taliesin's name would go on to be known across Britain, celebrated as one of the greatest poets and seers who ever lived.

Top: *The Magic Circle*, 1886. Painter John William Waterhouse's depiction of a Celtic sorceress, usually taken to be Ceridwen. **Above:** Elffin discovers the infant Taliesin. Painting, circa mid-19th-century, artist unknown.

CHAPTER THREE

CORNISH MYTHOLOGY

3

Cornwall shares its ancient cultural heritage with its Brythonic cousins Brittany and Wales, as well as Ireland and parts of England. Rich with tales of giants, mermaids, and adventure, Cornish myths reflect the deep connection between the ancient Cornish people and their rugged, coastal landscape

Opposite: The glorious and craggy Cornish coastline at the Bedruthan Steps in Cornwall. Cornish mythology relates directly to Welsh, and also Irish myths, and of course shares the roots of, and many of the legendary locations of, Arthurian Legend.

THE LEGEND OF TRISTAN AND ISEULT

The story of Tristan and Iseult begins with a young knight named Tristan, a nephew of King Mark of Cornwall...

Above: *Tristan and Isolde, or, The End of the Song* by Edmund Leighton, 1902; **Top:** *Tristan and Isolde, the Tragedy* by Rogelio de Egusquiza (1845-1915); **Opposite:** *Tristan and Isolde* by John Duncan, oil on canvas, 1912

Tristan was admired not only for his bravery but also for his musical talent and kind-hearted nature. Raised in the court of King Mark, he became the king's most loyal and beloved knight. His adventures took him far from Cornwall, and it was during one such journey that he became embroiled in events that would seal his fate.

King Mark had long wished for a politically advantageous marriage, and his chosen bride was Iseult, the beautiful daughter of the King of Ireland. The task of escorting the Irish princess safely to Cornwall fell to the trusted Tristan, who dutifully set out for Ireland.

Upon arriving in the Irish court, Tristan proved his valor by slaying a fearsome dragon that had long terrorized the land. This heroic act earned him the respect and gratitude of the Irish king, and Iseult was reluctantly given over for her impending marriage to Mark.

Before leaving Ireland, however, a mistake was made—one that would forever change the lives of Tristan and Iseult. Iseult's mother, wishing to ensure her daughter's happiness in her arranged marriage, prepared a love potion. The potion was intended for Iseult and King Mark to drink together on their wedding night, sealing their union with an eternal bond

of love. However, during the voyage back to Cornwall, Tristan and Iseult, unaware of the potion's true nature, mistakenly consumed it. The effect of the potion was immediate and profound. Tristan and Iseult were overwhelmed with a love so powerful that it erased all thoughts of duty or loyalty to King Mark. The magic created an irresistible bond between them, and they became deeply and irrevocably in love. Though they both understood the danger of their feelings and the betrayal it represented to King Mark, they found themselves unable to resist the powerful enchantment. They pledged themselves to each other, bound by a force they could not control. Upon arriving in Cornwall, Iseult was reluctantly wed to King Mark, as had been arranged. Yet despite their best efforts to hide their feelings, Tristan and Iseult could not keep their love a secret for long. They began to meet in secret, slipping away from the castle to be together. Rumors spread throughout the court, and suspicion grew.

King Mark, initially unaware, came to suspect that his new wife and his beloved nephew were hiding something from him.

Above: *Tristan and Isolde*, by Herbert James Draper, 1901; **Top, left:** *Tristan and Isolde Sharing the Potion*, by John William Waterhouse, 1916. Private collection; **Main image, top right:** *Tristan and Isolde*, a modern fantasy digital work by Luccio Darezzo, on DeviantArt

The king was torn; he had great affection for both Tristan and Iseult, but he could not tolerate betrayal.

As time went on, the affair became harder to conceal. King Mark's courtiers, eager to gain favor, began to report the couple's clandestine meetings. Eventually, the king confronted them. Despite his anger and sense of betrayal, Mark still cared for both Tristan and Iseult. He did not want to see them executed, so he sought a different form of justice. He banished Tristan from Cornwall, sending him away in hopes that the separation would break the bond between the two lovers.

Tristan, now exiled, wandered across Britain and eventually made his way to Brittany, where he tried to start anew. There, he met and married another woman named Iseult—often called Iseult of the White Hands. Though she was kind and gentle, Tristan's heart remained with Iseult of Cornwall. His marriage was one of obligation, not love, and he was unable to forget the deep connection forged by the potion.

He frequently thought of Iseult of Cornwall and longed to return to her. Back in Cornwall, Iseult struggled with her own feelings. She remained loyal to her husband, King Mark, and tried to fulfill

THE CELTIC WORLD
Richard Wagner's *Tristan und Isolde*

Ancient and distant Celtic mythology, and its subsequent re-writing in the early medieval period, suffuses 19th-century European culture (along with a concurrent revival of the Norse and proto-Germanic peoples). Fostered principally by several 12th-century figures: English historian Geoffrey of Monmouth, the French epic poet Chrétien de Troyes, and the Germans Wolfram (von Eschenbach) and Gottfried (von Strassburg), the distant Celtic legends were re-inscribed by Christianity into the Arthurian chivalric code, and the ideals of courtly love. By the 19th-century, artists and composers throughout Europe were interpreting these old, re-written myths. German Romantic composer Richard Wagner manifested his enduring art through his obsession with Viking sagas and his *Tristan und Isolde* and *Parzifal* (see page 213) works. His masterpieces expressed his vision of orchestral theater.

Far left: A portrait of the German Romantic composer Richard Wagner, circa 1870s; **Left:** A performance of Wagner's *Tristan und Isolde*, Act III, final scene, by the Municipal Theatre, Dusseldorf, circa 1900

her duties as queen. However, her love for Tristan endured, and she too dreamed of reuniting with him. The lovers' separation was marked by loneliness and sorrow, each unable to move on from the other despite the circumstances that kept them apart.

Meanwhile, danger was never far from Tristan, who continued his life as a knight, engaging in battles and seeking out new adventures. During one such endeavor, he was grievously wounded, a wound that no healer seemed able to cure. Desperate, Tristan sent for Iseult of Cornwall, believing that only she possessed the skills and the love to save him. He arranged for a ship to bring her to Brittany, and a signal was devised: if the ship returned with Iseult, its sails would be white, and if she did not come, the sails would be black.

As Tristan lay dying, he awaited the ship's return, filled with hope that he would see his beloved one last time. When the ship finally appeared on the horizon, his wife, Iseult of the White Hands, saw it first. Out of jealousy and heartbreak over her husband's undying love for another, she lied to Tristan, telling him that the sails were black. Tristan, overwhelmed with despair, believed that Iseult of Cornwall had abandoned him. He closed his eyes and succumbed to his injuries, his heart broken and his spirit crushed.

When Iseult of Cornwall finally arrived, it was too late. She found Tristan lifeless, his spirit already departed. Stricken with grief, she lay beside him, unable to bear the weight of her loss.

The legends say that she died there, her heart shattered by sorrow. The lovers were buried together, and it is said that two trees grew from their graves, intertwining their branches in a final symbol of their eternal love.

Above: An early-20th-century illustration by Arthur Rackham from the original Cornish Celtic legend of *Tristan and Iseult*—note the name spelling in many of thes captions—Modern academics almost always refer to this story using the 12th-century construction of the original Irish princess's name: Isolde.

THE GIANTS OF CORNWALL

Cornwall, a land of rugged coastlines and mysterious landscapes, is home to numerous legends of giants that have been passed down through generations.

Top left: The Giant's House, Trethevy Quoit megalithic standing stone tomb, near St. Cleer, Cornwall. The construction has been dated to circa 4,000 BC; **Top right:** The death of the giant Cormoran. Children's book illustration by R. Doyle in *The Story of Jack and the Giants*, London, 1851; **Above:** The Giant's Quoits, Rosenithon, Cornwall

These giants are believed to have once roamed the hills and valleys of Cornwall, shaping its landscape with their tremendous strength and leaving behind tales of heroism, rivalry, and tragedy. The stories of the Cornish giants are central to the mythology of the region, reflecting the powerful and untamed nature of the Cornish landscape, as well as the cultural identity of the Cornish people.

Origins and Characteristics

The giants of Cornwall are ancient beings whose stories are rooted in Celtic and pre-Celtic traditions. They are typically portrayed as immense figures, possessing both great physical power and a penchant for mischief or outright hostility toward humans. These giants were often considered protectors of their territories, fiercely guarding their lands against any perceived intrusion. At the same time, they could also be playful, engaging in contests of strength or showing a surprising sense of camaraderie.

Cornish giants are distinct from other giants found in Celtic mythology. They are often associated with specific landmarks, such as hills, stones, and natural formations, which are believed to have been created by the giants themselves. According to local legends, many of Cornwall's rocky outcrops and

large boulders were thrown by the giants during their quarrels or used by them to mark their territory. Their colossal size and strength were integral to their characterization, and their connection to the landscape reinforces their presence as part of the land itself.

Notable Giants

One of the most famous giants in Cornish folklore is Cormoran, who was said to inhabit St. Michael's Mount, an island off the southern coast of Cornwall. Cormoran is often depicted as a fearsome and greedy giant, known for terrorizing the local people. According to legend, Cormoran would come ashore to steal cattle and other livestock from nearby villages.

His reign of terror continued until he was outwitted by a young boy named Jack, who later became known as Jack the Giant Killer. Jack dug a deep pit and lured Cormoran into it, trapping the giant and ending his tyranny. This tale is one of the most well-known stories from Cornish folklore and has contributed significantly to the legend of the giant-slaying hero.

Another notable giant is Wrath, who was said to live on the Rame Peninsula. Wrath, unlike Cormoran, is depicted as more of a tragic figure. He was known for his love of the land and his desire to protect it. According to legend, Wrath fought against other giants who tried to invade his territory, but he was eventually defeated. His death is said to have caused a great storm that reshaped the peninsula, leaving behind a landscape that still bears the scars of the giants' battles.

Trecobben, another giant associated with Cornish mythology, is linked to Trencrom Hill. Trecobben was known for his rivalry with Cormoran, and the two giants would throw enormous boulders at each other across the countryside. The boulders that can still be found scattered across the region are said to be remnants of their fierce battles.

Main image, top: The Giant's Stone in Zennor, Cornwall, Photographed in 1911 by Herbert Hughes. Courtesy of The Royal Cornwall Museum; **Above:** Jack killing the giant, from *The Chronicle of the Valiant Feats of Jack the Giant Killer*, 1845

The story of the Mermaid of Zennor takes place in the small village of Zennor, located on the rugged coast of Cornwall.

THE MERMAID OF ZENNOR

Above: The Mermaid Chair in St. Senara's church Zennor, Cornwall; **Opposite, top left:** A contemporary relief/letterpress print of the Mermaid of Zennor by Sarah Young, available on Etsy; **Opposite, center left:** Close-up of the Mermaid Chair carving in St. Senara's

In the village stands the old church of St. Senara, where the villagers would gather each Sunday for worship. Among the congregation, there was a young man named Mathew Trewella, known for his handsome looks and his beautiful singing voice. His voice was so enchanting that people would often attend services just to hear him sing.

One day, a mysterious visitor appeared at the church—a beautiful woman whom no one had ever seen before. She had long, flowing golden hair and wore clothes of an unusual and shimmering fabric that seemed to glisten like the sea. The villagers were entranced by her beauty, but none more so than Mathew.

Week after week, she returned to the church, always sitting quietly in the back pew, her eyes fixed on Mathew as he sang. Mathew, equally captivated, felt an inexplicable attraction to the stranger. Her presence seemed to fill the church with a sense of wonder, as if the sea itself had found its way inside.

One evening, after the service had ended, Mathew followed her as she left the church and headed toward the cliffs that overlooked the ocean. The woman, aware of his presence, led him to the rocky shore. As she reached the water's edge, she revealed her true identity: she was a mermaid, a creature of the sea.

Her name was Morveren, and she had been drawn to Zennor by Mathew's beautiful voice, a sound unlike anything she had heard beneath the waves. Morveren invited Mathew to join her in the sea, and so great was his love for her that he willingly followed. Hand in hand, they disappeared into the ocean, never to be seen again by the villagers of Zennor.

In the days that followed, the people of Zennor searched for Mathew, but he was nowhere to be found. The only clue to his fate was the strange figure that some claimed to have seen sitting on the rocks at the edge of the sea—a mermaid, gazing out toward the village with a look of longing in her eyes. From that time on, the legend of the Mermaid of Zennor became part of the village's history. It is said that on quiet nights, if you listen closely by the shore, you can still hear the hauntingly beautiful sound of Mathew's singing, carried on the breeze from beneath the waves.

Above: *The Mermaid of Zennor*, a 1900 watercolor by John Reinhard Weguelin, a British painter. The Mermaid of Zennor was an enduring Cornish folk tale of a mermaid who lived at Pendour Cove, near Zennor on the North Cornwall coast. The story was first documented by the Cornish folklorist William Bottrell in 1873. The young man in the picture is Matthew Trewhell, a chorister of St. Senara's church in Zennor, with whose voice the mermaid was besotted. According to legend, he fell in love with the mermaid and went to share her watery home, although his voice can still be heard at Pendour Cove when he is singing.

Lyonesse, also known as the Lost Land of Lyonesse, is a legendary sunken kingdom said to lie off the coast of Cornwall, between Land's End and the Isles of Scilly.

Above left: The Lady Lyonesse questions Sir Beaumains's dwarf & finds out that the knight is the son of a king, and his true identity is Sir Gareth of Orkney; **Above right:** The Armed Knight Rock and Longships Lighthouse, from Land's End, the South-Westernmost point of the mainland of England. The Armed Knight rock area is associated with Arthurian legend and the lost land of Lyonesse, which sank beneath the waves while its heir, Tristan, was at his uncle Mark's court in Cornwall.

Often compared to Atlantis, Lyonesse is a significant element of Cornish mythology, shrouded in tales of tragedy, enchantment, and a deep connection to both Arthurian legend and Cornish cultural identity. The stories of Lyonesse have been passed down for centuries, weaving together elements of history, folklore, and the mysterious power of the sea.

MYTHOLOGICAL BACKGROUND

Lyonesse is often depicted as a prosperous kingdom that existed along the southwestern coast of Britain. According to legend, Lyonesse was a fertile land, blessed with verdant fields, thriving villages, and majestic castles. It was said to be home to a noble people, including some of the most famous figures in Arthurian legend. One of the most notable associations is with Tristan, the tragic hero of the tale of Tristan and Isolde. Tristan is believed to have been born in Lyonesse, and his connection to the lost land further ties its mythology to the broader body of Arthurian tales.

The fall of Lyonesse is described as a sudden and catastrophic event, occurring on a day when the sea rose without warning, swallowing the kingdom and all its inhabitants. The reasons for this calamity vary depending on the version of the story. Some accounts suggest that the kingdom's fall was a divine punishment for the people's wickedness or a great battle that had gone against the natural order. Other versions imply that the disaster was simply a natural catastrophe, a powerful storm or earthquake that caused the land to sink beneath the waves. In the most popular version of the myth, only one man survived the disaster—Trevelyan, who managed to escape on a swift white

LYONESSE

horse. Trevelyan rode furiously ahead of the advancing sea, and it is said that he barely reached the safety of higher ground before the entire kingdom disappeared beneath the water. From that day forward, Lyonesse was no more, and the sea reclaimed its once-thriving lands.

PHYSICAL TRACES AND FOLKLORE

The legend of Lyonesse has persisted for centuries, and even today, traces of the lost land are said to linger in Cornish folklore. Fishermen in the area have long told tales of underwater forests, submerged buildings, and the faint sound of church bells that can be heard on quiet days, carried across the water from beneath the waves.

The Isles of Scilly, a group of small islands off the coast of Cornwall, are often thought to be the remaining hilltops of Lyonesse, the only parts of the land that were not submerged. Historical records from the medieval period contain various references to the lost kingdom. Chroniclers such as Geoffrey of Monmouth included mentions of sunken lands and kingdoms that align with the concept of Lyonesse, further adding to its mystique. While these records are not considered factual, they have served to keep the story alive, blurring the lines between history, legend, and the cultural imagination.

There is also a geological element to the legend. The area between Land's End and the Isles of Scilly is known to be relatively shallow, and during extremely low tides, large expanses of sandbanks are revealed. This has led some to speculate that the idea of a sunken kingdom may have originated from real observations of changing coastal landscapes and the remnants of ancient submerged structures. However, the exact nature of Lyonesse remains a mystery, with no definitive archaeological evidence to support its existence.

Main image: St. Michael's Mount, Cornwall, by Alfred Quinton, circa 1920. Legend has it that it was part of the drowned land of Lyonesse, where King Arthur & his knights rode. It's also considered the starting point for the St. Michael's Mount, Glastonbury, and Lowestoft leyline; **Above:** Bant's Carn is a Bronze Age entrance grave on the island of St. Mary's in the Isles of Scilly, England. The tomb is one of the best examples of a Scillonian entrance grave. Below Bant's Carn lie the remains of the Iron Age village of Halangy Down.

JACK THE GIANT KILLER

The legend of Jack the Giant Killer is one of Cornwall's most famous and enduring myths, recounting the adventures of a brave and clever young man named Jack, who rises from humble origins to become a celebrated hero.

Top left: "Pollock's Scenes in Jack the Giant Killer," published in Hoxton, London in 1870. This plate is one of a series made for a children's Toy Theatre. By the Victorian age, Cornish mythology had long since degenerated into nursery stories, and the distinctly English pantomime tradition; **Top right:** Circa 1900s illustration from the book *Jack the Giant Killer*; **Opposite, top left:** "The giant Cormoran was the terror of all the country-side," from Jack the Giant Killer in *English Fairy Tales*, illustration by Arthur Rackham, circa 1920s; **Opposite, top right:** Printed illustration from an 1865 edition of *Jack the Giant Killer*; **Opposite, bottom right:** Jack administers the *coup de grâce* to a Cornish giant in this 1872 English woodcut

Jack's exploits are set in the days of King Arthur and are marked by his encounters with fearsome giants that terrorized the land. The story begins in Cornwall, where Jack lived as a young farmer's son. At that time, the land was plagued by a giant named Cormoran, who lived on St. Michael's Mount, an island off the coast of Cornwall.

Cormoran was a vicious creature who frequently descended from his island lair to raid the nearby villages, stealing cattle, crops, and even people. The villagers lived in constant fear of the giant, unable to defend themselves against his immense strength.

Jack, known for his wit and courage, decided to rid the land of this terror. He devised a clever plan to trick the giant. One night, he took a shovel and dug a deep pit in the path leading to Cormoran's lair. He then covered the pit with branches and straw to disguise it. At dawn, Jack blew a horn to wake the giant, who charged down the mountain, enraged by the disturbance. As Cormoran rushed

toward Jack, he fell into the hidden pit. While the giant was trapped and unable to escape, Jack killed him with a blow to the head.

For his bravery, Jack was hailed as a hero, and he earned the name "Jack the Giant Killer." The king of Cornwall rewarded him with a sword, a belt, and a purse of gold, making Jack a man of both wealth and fame.

After his first victory, Jack's reputation spread, and he soon faced more giants in his adventures. One of his next encounters was with Blunderbore, a cruel giant who lived in a castle and had captured many knights and fair maidens, keeping them imprisoned in his dungeons. Jack, determined to free the prisoners, set out for Blunderbore's castle. Along the way, he met another giant, Thunderdell, and used his quick thinking to outwit both giants. Jack arrived at Blunderbore's castle and found himself in the giants' clutches, but using his cunning, he tricked them into capturing each other.

Blunderbore and Thunderdell ended up ensnared by their own traps, and Jack slew them both, freeing the prisoners and claiming the giants' treasure. His reputation as a fearless giant-slayer grew even more.

In another of Jack's exploits, he defeated Galligantus, a giant sorcerer who had enchanted a beautiful princess. Jack used a magic cap, shoes, and sword given to him by a group of grateful knights he had previously saved. With these magical items, Jack was able to defeat Galligantus and break the enchantment, freeing the princess, who later became his wife.

BRETON MYTHOLOGY

4

Breton mythology, deeply rooted in the traditions and folklore of Brittany, weaves together ancient Celtic paganism and later Christian influences into a rich and multifaceted tapestry. Shaped by the region's Celtic heritage and seafaring culture, these stories preserve echoes of ancient beliefs that have evolved through the centuries

Opposite: The wild, primeval coast of the Brittany peninsula at Pointe du Millier, France

As one of the six Celtic nations, Brittany (or *Breizh* in Breton) shares a common cultural heritage with regions such as Ireland, Wales, and Cornwall, but its myths and legends are shaped by the unique history and geography of the Breton peninsula.

The rugged coastline, deep forests, and mystical landscapes of Brittany provide the backdrop for many of its legendary tales, which feature gods, fairies, heroes, and magical beings that still resonate in Breton culture today.

CELTIC ORIGINS AND CHRISTIAN INFLUENCE

The foundation of Breton mythology lies in the ancient Celtic beliefs brought to Brittany by the migration of Britons from the island of Great Britain during the early medieval period. This migration occurred as the Roman Empire was collapsing and Saxon invaders began to encroach on the Britons' lands. The Britons brought with them their language, culture, and myths, which took root in the Armorican peninsula, influencing the folklore and oral traditions of the region.

As in other Celtic mythologies, the deities of Breton tradition are closely connected to nature, particularly the sea and the land. The ancient Celts believed in a pantheon of gods and goddesses who controlled the forces of nature and guided human fate. However, as Christianity spread through Brittany in the early Middle Ages, these pagan beliefs began to blend with Christian doctrine. This process of syncretization led to the transformation of many old deities and spirits into Christian saints or figures within Christian morality tales. Some myths were adapted or reinterpreted to fit within a Christian worldview, but the underlying Celtic themes of heroism, magic, and the supernatural persisted.

KEY FIGURES AND THEMES

Breton mythology is populated by a wide variety of supernatural beings and legendary figures. Among the most important are Korrigans, small, fairy-like creatures who inhabit the forests, meadows, and waters of Brittany. These mischievous beings are often associated with the

Otherworld, a common theme in Celtic myth where the boundary between the mortal world and the spirit world is thin. Korrigans are known for both helping and hindering humans, depending on how they are treated.

Another central figure in Breton myth is the Ankou, a personification of death who rides a black cart, collecting the souls of the dead. The Ankou is often portrayed as a skeletal figure and is a remnant of the ancient Celtic belief in the importance of the afterlife and the journey of the soul.

Legends of lost cities and sunken lands, such as the famous city of Ys, also feature prominently in Breton mythology. These tales often reflect the region's deep connection to the sea and the dangers it poses. The sea is both a giver and a taker in Breton lore, a source of life but also of destruction.

ORAL TRADITION AND CULTURAL LEGACY

Breton mythology has been passed down primarily through oral tradition, with storytellers, or conteurs, playing a key role in preserving and sharing these tales. While written accounts of these myths exist, it is the spoken word, songs, and ballads that have kept Breton legends alive in the collective memory of the people. Festivals and local traditions continue to honor these ancient stories, and many place names and landmarks in Brittany are connected to mythical figures and events.

Above: The Standing Stones, *Alignments de Kerlescan*, at Carnac, Brittany; **Top:** Coastal walking trail, Brittany; **Opposite:** Map of Brittany, circa 1634

THE LEGEND OF YS

In the ancient kingdom of Armorica, where the land met the sea in a wild embrace, the legendary city of Ys was built by Gradlon, King of Cornouaille...

Above: Rocher du Roi Gradlon, Pointe de Pern, Ouessant Island, Finistere, Brittany; **Top:** "The Escape of King Gradlon from the Flooded City of Ys," in *Legends and Romances of Brittany*, edited by Lewis Spence, 1917

Ys was a marvel, a city of unmatched beauty and wealth, constructed on land reclaimed from the sea by the engineering prowess of Gradlon's daughter, the Princess Dahut. The city's walls stood tall and impenetrable, with a grand gate designed to keep the ever-encroaching sea at bay. Only King Gradlon had the key to this gate, which was used to open the walls during low tide and let the sea flow in and out.

Dahut, however, was not content with the order and peace that her father sought to maintain. She grew increasingly wild and restless, indulging in a life of pleasure and excess. Dahut turned Ys into a city of revelry, where nights were filled with feasts, celebrations, and dark magic. It is said that she had become a disciple of the powers of darkness, forsaking the gods her father revered. Under her influence, Ys became a place where virtue was abandoned, and decadence reigned.

One fateful night, during a grand festival, a mysterious stranger appeared in Ys. He was handsome, seductive, and cloaked in an aura of danger. Captivated by his charm, Dahut invited him to her private chambers. The stranger, whom many believed to be the devil himself in disguise, convinced Dahut to steal the key to the city's sea gate from her father.

Tempted by his promises of even greater power and pleasure, Dahut obeyed.

As the city slept, Dahut crept into her father's chambers and took the key. With her guest by her side, she opened the gate, allowing the sea to pour into the city. The waters surged through the streets, quickly flooding the homes and palaces of Ys. The people awoke in terror as the once-safe walls of Ys could no longer hold back the fury of the ocean. Chaos erupted as the sea swallowed the city.

King Gradlon, sensing the disaster, rushed to Dahut's side, realizing too late what she had done. He took her in his arms and fled the city on his magical horse, Morvarc'h, whose hooves could ride over water. The waves rose higher, threatening to drag them both into the depths.

As they rode, a voice—some say it was that of a divine figure, perhaps Saint Gwénnolé, who had warned Gradlon of Ys's doom—called out to the king. The voice demanded that he cast Dahut into the sea to save himself. Torn by the love for his daughter but knowing he had no other choice, Gradlon pushed Dahut from the horse's back into the raging waters. As soon as Dahut was taken by the sea, the waves calmed, and Gradlon was able to escape to safety.

The city of Ys was lost forever beneath the ocean, becoming a drowned city whose ruins were said to be visible beneath the waves on clear days. Some say Dahut transformed into a mermaid, cursed to live in the waters she once ruled.

Above: *The Baptism of Clovis in Reims* in 496 made him the only Gallic Christian king and won him increased support from his former Roman subjects in Gaul. Painting by François-Louis Dejuinne, 1837. Sourced from The History Files; **Top, main image:** *La Fuite de Roi Gradlon*, by Évariste Vital Luminai, 1884. Musée des Beaux Arts, Quimper, Brittany, France. A similar version is titled *The Flight of St. Guénolé and King Gradlon*, also by Luminai. He was known as "the Painter of the Gauls." Courtesy WikiCommons

KORRIGANS

Korrigans are mythical creatures from Breton folklore, often described as mischievous, magical beings akin to fairies or elves. Rooted in the cultural traditions of Brittany, these creatures inhabit forests, rivers, and meadows, embodying the mysterious and untamed aspects of the natural world.

Korrigans have an ambiguous nature, both benevolent and malevolent, depending on how they are treated by humans. Their stories reflect the deep ties that Breton people have with the land and the belief in the enchantments hidden within the natural environment.

PHYSICAL DESCRIPTION AND TRAITS

Korrigans are typically depicted as small, humanoid beings, standing only a few feet tall. Their appearance is often enchanting, with beautiful faces and long, flowing hair that can change color, particularly glowing silver in the moonlight. However, their beauty can be deceptive, as they are said to transform into hideous forms when angered or threatened. This dual nature symbolizes the thin line between beauty and danger in the natural world. Korrigans are often seen wearing garments made from natural materials like moss, leaves, or the bark of trees, blending seamlessly into their woodland surroundings. Their nature is not merely whimsical; they possess supernatural powers, including the ability to change their shape, become invisible, or hypnotize unwary travelers. These powers, combined with their unpredictable temperament, make them both respected and feared by those who come into contact with them. They are often portrayed as nocturnal creatures, becoming most active at twilight or under the moonlight, which adds to their association with magic and mystery.

ROLE IN BRETON FOLKLORE

Korrigans play a significant role in Breton mythology, often embodying the unpredictability of the natural world. They are known for their enchanting voices, and their songs are said to lure travelers into the depths of the forest, where they may become lost or fall under the Korrigans' spell. In many tales, they are depicted as guardians of sacred springs and wells, places considered highly magical in Celtic tradition. These sacred sites, often linked to the worship of ancient deities, were seen as portals to the otherworld, with Korrigans serving as their protectors. Their ambivalent attitude toward humans is a recurring theme. They are known to be kind and generous to those who show them respect, offering gifts or assistance to people who take care not to disturb their homes or sacred spaces. However, those who are careless or disrespectful—by polluting their waters, cutting down sacred trees, or mocking them—are likely to incur their wrath. Such individuals may be cursed, bewitched, or led astray in the wilderness, unable to find their way home.

Above: *Traveller Assailed by Korrigans*, metal etching, possibly by the French painter, book and magazine illustrator André Castaigne, 1897

THE ANKOU

The Ankou is a prominent figure in Breton folklore, often depicted as the personification of death.

Rooted in the myths of Brittany, a region in northwestern France, the Ankou serves as a harbinger of mortality, appearing as a ghostly figure whose primary role is to gather the souls of the deceased. Its significance in Breton culture is substantial, representing the ever-present link between the living and the inevitability of death. This dark, mysterious figure is often portrayed in tales that reflect the region's somber views on the afterlife and the inescapable nature of fate.

DESCRIPTION AND CHARACTERISTICS

The Ankou is traditionally envisioned as a tall, skeletal figure, often cloaked in black and carrying a scythe, much like the stereotypical Grim Reaper. Its scythe, however, is often said to be turned backwards, adding a distinct touch to the Breton conception of death. The Ankou is also frequently accompanied by a rickety cart known as the "Karriguel an Ankou," which is used to carry the souls of those who have recently died. Some accounts describe him as wearing a wide-brimmed hat that conceals his gaunt, spectral face.

There are differing descriptions of the Ankou's identity. In some versions, he is believed to be the spirit of the last person to die in a given year, chosen to act as the collector of souls until someone else dies at the end of the next year. This cyclical nature of the Ankou's role serves to emphasize the unbroken chain of life and death, a key theme in Breton folk belief.

ORIGINS AND MYTHOLOGICAL CONTEXT

The origins of the Ankou are deeply rooted in Celtic mythology, with parallels found in other personifications of death throughout Celtic cultures, such as the Irish "Banshee" or the Welsh "Gwrach-y-Rhibyn." The concept of an entity that escorts souls to the afterlife is common across Celtic traditions, highlighting the belief in a close relationship between the physical and spiritual worlds.

The Ankou, however, is unique in that he is not inherently malevolent; his role is not to harm but to act as a guide, embodying the inevitability of death without cruelty or malice.

Breton folklore presents the Ankou as an inescapable figure whose presence is a constant reminder of mortality. His cart, often heard creaking in the dead of night, serves as a warning to those who hear it—an omen that death is near. The association with rural life, dark forests, and remote villages is also significant, reflecting the harsh realities of Breton peasant life and their close connection to the natural cycles of birth, growth, and decay.

Above: The Ankou, the harbinger of death, the collector of souls. Stone carving on the exterior of Notre Dame de Bulat church, Bulat Pestivien, Cotes d'Armor, Brittany

ARTHURIAN LEGEND

5

Arthurian legend emerges from the misty landscapes of medieval Britain and France, forming a timeless realm of enchantment, valor, and moral complexity. Rooted in Celtic myth and medieval romance, these stories are steeped in the ideals of an imagined golden age, where loyalty and love often clash with ambition and betrayal

Opposite: Down the centuries, Glastonbury Tor has become *the* definitive location of the Isle of Avalon, where Arthur is brought by boat after his fatal last battle. In prehistory, the Tor, situated in the Somerset Levels, was an actual island, and during the Roman Occupation of Britain, sea salt was dried from the Levels' many marshlands. Successive draining and reclaiming for agricultural use over the last 1500 years has left it surrounded by fields. Its spiritual (and supernatural) legacy in Arthurian legend ensures that people from around the world come to explore the land and the legend of King Arthur.

The roots of Arthurian legend can be traced back to early medieval Britain, in the period following the complete Roman withdrawal from the British Isles around 409 AD.

Above: The ruins of Tintagel Castle, on the North Cornwall coast, Southwest England. The castle has a long association with legends related to King Arthur, which were first documented in the 12th century, when Geoffrey of Monmouth described Tintagel as the place of Arthur's conception in his spurious account of British history, *Historia Regum Britanniae*. A tourist destination since the mid-19th century, today the castle is in the possession of William, Prince of Wales, as part of the Royal landholdings of the Duchy of Cornwall. The site is managed by English Heritage.

Arthurian legend is one of the most enduring and influential bodies of mythology in Western culture, weaving together tales of heroism, chivalry, magic, and romance. Centered around the figure of King Arthur, the legendary ruler of Britain, and his knights of the Round Table, these stories have evolved over centuries, blending historical elements with myth and folklore to create a rich tapestry of narrative that has captivated audiences for generations.

ORIGINS AND HISTORICAL CONTEXT

The roots of Arthurian legend can be traced back to early medieval Britain, during the period following the Roman withdrawal from the island. This was a time of great upheaval, as various tribes and kingdoms vied for control. The earliest references to Arthur appear in Welsh and Breton sources, where he is depicted as a heroic figure leading the Britons against invading Saxons. These early mentions, however, are brief and lack the detailed narrative that would later define Arthurian legend.

It was not until the 12th century, with the writings of Geoffrey of Monmouth in his *Historia Regum Britanniae* (*The History of the Kings of Britain*), that the figure of Arthur began to take on the form recognizable today. Geoffrey's work, a mix

of history, legend, and invention—and, of course, the weaving in of Christianity—presented Arthur as a great king who united Britain, established a glorious court at Camelot, and led his knights in battles both earthly and otherworldly. This account laid the foundation for the vast body of literature that would follow.

KEY THEMES AND MOTIFS

Arthurian legend is characterized by several recurring themes and motifs that have become central to the narrative. The Christian concept of chivalry and the knightly code is paramount, with the knights of the Round Table embodying ideals of bravery, honor, and loyalty. These knights, including Sir Lancelot, Sir Gawain, and Sir Galahad, undertake quests that test their character and strength, such as the search for the Holy Grail, a symbol of divine grace and the ultimate spiritual quest.

Magic and the supernatural are also integral to Arthurian legend. Merlin, the enigmatic wizard and advisor to Arthur, plays a crucial role in shaping the events of the narrative. Other mystical elements include the Lady of the Lake, who bestows the sword Excalibur upon Arthur, and the isle of Avalon, a place of healing and mystery where Arthur is taken after his final battle.

The theme of betrayal is another important aspect of the legend. The tragic love affair between Lancelot and Queen Guinevere, Arthur's wife, leads to the downfall of Camelot, highlighting the fragile nature of even the greatest of kingdoms. The treachery of Mordred, Arthur's illegitimate son, further contributes to the king's demise, culminating in the Battle of Camlann, where Arthur meets his end.

Top left, main image: The frontispiece from *The Romance of King Arthur and his Knights of the Round Table*, abridged from Sir Thomas Malory's *Morte d'Arthur* by Alfred W. Pollard. Illustrated by Arthur Rackham, and published In New York by Macmillan, 1920; **Top right:** *Guinevere*, circa late 19th-century; **Above:** *Voyage of King Arthur and Morgan Le Fay to the Isle of Avalon*, by Frank William Warwick Topham, 1888

Above left: Merlin guides King Arthur around the grounds of Camelot, in this circa 1868 wood engraving by Gustave Doré, the prolific French printmaker, painter and sculptor. He was frequently called upon by London publishers. Here, he was commissioned to illustrate an edition of Alfred, Lord Tennyson's epic poem *Idylls of the King*, published between 1859 and 1885; **Above right:** *King Arthur*, a 1903 painting by Charles Ernest Butler RA. Butler specialized in landscapes and mythological scenes.

King Arthur is one of the most iconic figures in Western mythology, symbolizing the ideal of a noble and just ruler. As the legendary king of Britain, Arthur's story is a blend of history, myth, and folklore, forming the foundation of the rich tapestry of tales known as the Arthurian legend. His life and reign are marked by his establishment of the Round Table, his quest to unify his kingdom, his tragic flaws, and his ultimate downfall.

HISTORICAL ORIGINS

The historical basis for King Arthur is a subject of much debate among scholars. While some believe that Arthur may have been a real figure, possibly a Romano-British leader who defended Britain against Saxon invaders in the late 5th and early 6th centuries, there is no definitive evidence to confirm his existence. The earliest references

As the legendary King of Britain, Arthur's story is a blend of history, myth, and folklore, forming the foundation of the rich tapestry of tales known as the Arthurian legend.

KING ARTHUR

to Arthur appear in Welsh and Breton sources, where he is portrayed as a heroic warrior. However, it was not until the 12th century, with Geoffrey of Monmouth's *Historia Regum Britanniae* (*The History of the Kings of Britain*), that Arthur became a central figure in British legend, depicted as a king who united the land and established a golden age of chivalry.

THE LEGEND OF ARTHUR

According to legend, Arthur was the son of Uther Pendragon, the king of Britain, and Igraine, the wife of the Duke of Cornwall. His birth was shrouded in mystery and magic, as Merlin, the great wizard, orchestrated the union of Uther and Igraine under unusual circumstances. To protect the newborn Arthur from the dangers of court intrigue, Merlin arranged for him to be raised in secret by Sir Ector, unaware of his royal lineage. Arthur's ascent to the throne is marked by the famous episode of the Sword in the Stone. When the king of Britain died without an heir, Merlin proclaimed that whoever could pull the sword from the stone would be the rightful king. Despite the attempts of many knights, only the young Arthur succeeded, revealing his true identity and fulfilling his destiny. This act solidified his claim to the throne and began his reign as king.

THE ROUND TABLE AND CHIVALRY

One of Arthur's most significant contributions to his kingdom was the establishment of the Round Table, a symbol of equality and unity among his knights. The Round Table was more than just a physical object; it represented the chivalric code that Arthur sought to uphold—a code that emphasized bravery, honor, loyalty, and justice. The knights who sat at the Round Table, including Sir Lancelot, Sir Gawain, and Sir Galahad, became legendary figures in their own right, undertaking quests that tested their virtues and often involved encounters with the supernatural.

ARTHUR'S DOWNFALL

Despite his achievements, Arthur's reign was fraught with personal and political challenges. The love affair between his queen, Guinevere, and his most trusted knight, Lancelot, sowed the seeds of discord within the kingdom. This betrayal, coupled with the treachery of Mordred—Arthur's illegitimate son—led to the downfall of Camelot. The final battle between Arthur and Mordred at Camlann resulted in the death of both men, marking the end of Arthur's reign and the disintegration of the fellowship of the Round Table.

Above: *Study for the Head of King Arthur*, William Dyce, 1855. William Dyce FRSE RSA RA was a Scottish painter who played a part in the formation of public art education in Britain—especially the South Kensington Schools, which became the Royal College of Art. Dyce was also acquainted with the artists of the Pre-Raphaelite Brotherhood and contributed to their early recognition.

MERLIN

Merlin stands as a pivotal figure within Arthurian legend, his presence shaping the very course of events that would define the mythical kingdom of Camelot.

Above: Merlin the Magician, by Louis Rhead for *The Story of King Arthur & His Knights* by Sir James Knowles, 1923; **Opposite:** Merlin the Wizard, handcolored woodcut, probably Gustave Doré, mid-to-late 19th-century

Known as a master of magic and prophecy, Merlin's influence extends far beyond his role as King Arthur's mentor, encompassing a vast array of mystical lore and ancient wisdom that bridges the mortal and supernatural realms.

Mysterious Beginnings

Merlin's origins are as mysterious as the man himself, with various accounts offering different interpretations of his birth and early life. The most widely accepted version of his origin story is that Merlin was the son of a mortal woman and an incubus, a demonic spirit. This unusual parentage endowed Merlin with extraordinary powers, including the ability to foresee the future, shape-shift, and perform powerful magic. Some versions of the legend suggest that Merlin was baptized at birth, which tempered his demonic nature and allowed him to use his powers for good.

Architect of Arthur's Destiny

Merlin's involvement in the legend of King Arthur is indispensable, as he is directly responsible for the events that lead to Arthur's rise. Acting as the guiding hand behind Arthur's conception, Merlin employed his magical prowess to disguise Uther Pendragon, Arthur's father, as Gorlois, the Duke of Cornwall, allowing Uther to be with Gorlois's wife, Igraine. This encounter resulted in Arthur's birth, fulfilling a prophecy that Britain's greatest king would emerge from these unusual circumstances. Aware of the dangers surrounding a child of such significance, Merlin took Arthur from his parents shortly after birth and arranged for him to be raised by Sir Ector, far from the intrigues of the court. Merlin's foresight ensured that Arthur grew up in relative obscurity, only to reveal his royal lineage when the time was right. The legendary episode of the Sword in the Stone was orchestrated by Merlin, who made certain that only Arthur could draw the sword, thus proving his right to the throne and setting the stage for his reign. During Arthur's rule, Merlin served not only as an advisor but also as a protector, guiding the young king through the complexities of leadership and the many challenges that arose. Merlin's wisdom and knowledge of both the natural and supernatural worlds allowed him to foresee threats and craft strategies that would ensure the stability of Arthur's kingdom.

The Enchanter's Fall

Merlin's downfall came as a result of his relationship with Vivian—also known as Nimue—the Lady of the Lake. Captivated by her beauty and charm, Merlin taught her many of his magical secrets, despite sensing the danger in doing so. Vivian, wary of Merlin's power, eventually used this knowledge against him, imprisoning him within a crystal cave or a tree, depending on the version of the story. Deprived of his freedom, Merlin's direct influence on the affairs of Camelot came to an end, leaving Arthur and his knights to face the kingdom's trials without his guidance.

GUINEVERE

As the wife of King Arthur and the queen of Camelot, Guinevere plays a crucial role in the stories that define the rise and fall of Arthur's kingdom.

Guinevere's character is complex, embodying both the ideals and the flaws that contribute to the eventual unraveling of the Round Table.

Origins and Marriage to Arthur

Most accounts place Guinevere as the daughter of King Leodegrance of Cameliard, although the specifics of her family tree are often vague and varied. Regardless of her background, Guinevere is consistently portrayed as a figure of great beauty, grace, and intelligence, qualities that made her the ideal consort for King Arthur. Guinevere's marriage to Arthur was not only a personal union but also a political alliance that strengthened Arthur's claim to the throne. According to many versions of the legend, their marriage was arranged by Merlin, who foresaw both the greatness and the challenges that would arise from this union. On their wedding day, Guinevere brought with her the Round Table as part of her dowry, a gift from her father that would become a symbol of Arthur's court and his ideals of equality and chivalry.

The Love Triangle: Guinevere, Lancelot, and Arthur

One of the most enduring and tragic aspects of Guinevere's story is her love affair with Sir Lancelot, Arthur's greatest knight and most trusted friend. The bond between Guinevere and Lancelot began as one of mutual admiration and respect, but it soon deepened into a passionate and forbidden love. This relationship is central to the Arthurian narrative, as it sets in motion a series of events that ultimately

led to the downfall of Camelot. Despite her love for Arthur, Guinevere's feelings for Lancelot were undeniable, and their affair became one of the most famous love triangles in literary history. Their relationship was fraught with tension and danger, as it violated the sacred codes of both marriage and knighthood. Lancelot's loyalty to Arthur was tested by his love for Guinevere, creating an internal conflict that would haunt both him and the queen. The affair was eventually discovered, leading to a catastrophic rift in Arthur's court. The revelation of Guinevere and Lancelot's betrayal divided the knights of the Round Table, many of whom were torn between their loyalty to Arthur and their admiration for Lancelot. This division weakened the unity of Camelot, making it vulnerable to external threats and internal dissent.

Guinevere's Fate

The affair between Guinevere and Lancelot played a significant role in the events that led to the fall of Camelot. After the affair was exposed, Guinevere was sentenced to be burned at the stake for her betrayal, a punishment that reflected the gravity of her crime in the eyes of Arthur and his court. However, Lancelot's love for Guinevere drove him to rescue her from execution, further escalating the conflict and leading to a civil war within Arthur's kingdom. Following the collapse of Camelot and the death of Arthur at the Battle of Camlann, Guinevere's life took a somber turn. In many versions of the legend, she chose to withdraw from the world, entering a convent to atone for her sins. Her final years were marked by penitence and reflection, as she sought redemption for the role she played in the tragedy that befell Camelot.

This page, top right: Guinevere as modern fantasy, from Old World Gods; **Both pictures opposite,** and **above:** British 1930s children's book illustrations of Guinevere and Arthur, including the marriage of King Arthur to Guinevere, (opposite, top right); **Main image, above left:** *The Dawn of Love: Lancelot and Guinevere*, an 1867 steel engraving, by Gustave Doré, for the edition of Alfred, Lord Tennyson's *The Idylls of the King*, published between 1859 and 1885

MORGAN LE FAY

Morgan le Fay is often depicted as a powerful sorceress. Her name, "le Fay," indicates her association with fairy-like or magical beings—as well as their capricious nature.

Above, left: Detail from *Morgan Le Fay*, by Edward Burne-Jones, 1862. In many versions of the legends, Morgan Le Fay is Arthur's half-sister; **Above, right:** *Morgan le Fay*, by Frederick Sandys, 1863; **Opposite, top left:** *Morgana Le Fay*, Anikó Salamon's art for the video game *King Arthur II: The Role-Playing Wargame*, 2012; **Opposite, bottom:** Detail from *The Last Sleep of Arthur in Avalon*, again by Edward Burne-Jones, features Morgan Le Fay. In the 1880s, after the deaths of many of his close friends, the artist suffered deep grief and mounting isolation, and retreated into making pictures from Arthurian legend, and until his death in 1898 obsessively painted the central characters in many scenes. Burne-Jones worked on this massive canvas (the depiction shows just the central part of the overall canvas) for the final 17 years of his life, and it's considered his *magnum opus*. It is on permanent display in the Ponce Museum of Art in Puerto Rico.

The character of Morgan appears in various medieval texts, with her origins potentially tracing back to earlier Celtic mythology, where she may have been connected to goddesses such as the Irish Morrígan or the Welsh Modron. In early Arthurian literature, Morgan is sometimes portrayed as a healer and a figure of great knowledge, but her character evolves significantly across different texts.

Role in Arthurian Legend

Morgan le Fay's role in Arthurian legend is multifaceted, and she is portrayed with varying degrees of malevolence or benevolence depending on the source. In some stories, she is depicted as a half-sister to King Arthur, the daughter of Arthur's mother, Igraine, and her first husband, Gorlois. As a member of the royal family, Morgan holds significant influence within the court. Her relationship with Arthur is complex, often marked by rivalry, yet she occasionally assists him in critical moments.

One of the earliest and most significant depictions of Morgan le Fay comes from Geoffrey of Monmouth's *Vita Merlini* (*Life of Merlin*), where she is presented as a healer and a ruler of the Isle of Avalon. Here, Morgan is a benevolent figure, skilled in the arts of healing, and it is to her care

that Arthur is brought after being mortally wounded in battle. This portrayal contrasts sharply with later depictions, where she is more frequently seen as a seductress and an antagonist.

Evolution into a Villainess

As Arthurian legend evolved, particularly in the later medieval romances, Morgan le Fay's character increasingly took on darker tones. In works such as Sir Thomas Malory's *Le Morte d'Arthur*, she is portrayed as a cunning and dangerous sorceress who often plots against Arthur and his knights. Her motivations in these stories are complex, often driven by a mixture of jealousy, revenge, and a desire for power. In *Le Morte d'Arthur*, Morgan le Fay is depicted as an adversary who seeks to undermine Arthur's reign by any means necessary. She uses her magical abilities to create illusions, manipulate others, and even attempts to steal Excalibur, Arthur's sword, in order to weaken him. Despite her antagonistic role, Morgan le Fay is not devoid of redeeming qualities; her care for her lover, Accolon, and her eventual reconciliation with Arthur hint at the layered nature of her character.

LADY OF THE LAKE
NIMUE

Known by several names, including Nimue and Viviane, the Lady of the Lake plays a pivotal role in the narrative, acting as both a benefactor and, at times, a manipulator of key events within the legend.

Nimue's character embodies the connection between the human world and the supernatural, often serving as a bridge between the two.

Origins and Identity

The Lady of the Lake is a powerful enchantress who resides in a mystical, otherworldly realm, typically a lake or a body of water that serves as a portal to her magical domain. This lake is usually portrayed as being hidden from the mortal world, accessible only to those whom the Lady wishes to reach. In some versions of the legend, she is portrayed as a fairy or a water spirit, while in others, she is a human woman who has gained immortality and magical powers. Her name, too, varies—she is known as Nimue, Viviane, or simply the Lady of the Lake, depending on the story. Despite these variations, the Lady of the Lake is consistently depicted as a figure of immense power and wisdom, closely associated with the magical elements of the Arthurian world.

Role in Arthurian Legend

The Lady of the Lake is perhaps best known for her role in bestowing the sword Excalibur upon King Arthur. According to the legend, after Arthur has become king, he is led by the wizard Merlin to a lake where he sees a hand emerge from the water, holding the fabled sword. The Lady of the Lake offers Excalibur to Arthur, and he accepts it, securing his right to rule and his connection to the mystical forces that support his reign.

In addition to giving Excalibur to Arthur, the Lady of the Lake also plays a crucial role in the life of Merlin, the legendary wizard. In some tales, she is Merlin's student, learning the secrets of magic from him, while in others,

she is his lover or companion. However, in many versions of the story, the relationship between Merlin and the Lady takes a dark turn. She eventually uses the knowledge she has gained to trap Merlin, imprisoning him within a tree, a cave, or beneath a stone, depending on the version. This act removes Merlin from the narrative, allowing the Lady of the Lake to wield significant power in his absence.

Protector and Mentor

The Lady of the Lake is also depicted as a protector and mentor to various knights of the Round Table. Most notably, she is the guardian of Sir Lancelot, one of Arthur's greatest knights. According to the legend, the Lady takes the infant Lancelot to her underwater realm after the death of his parents and raises him there, endowing him with the skills and virtues that make him an exemplary knight.

Opposite: *The Beguiling of Merlin* by Edward Burne-Jones, 1874, oil on canvas. The great magician is helpless as Nimue, the Lady of the Lake, enchants him. Burne-Jones, the artist, though born in Birmingham, England, was the son of a Welshman, and was associated with the Pre-Raphaelite Brotherhood in the 1870s and 1880s. He was a close working companion of the Arts & Crafts designer William Morris; **Top left:** Nimue traps Merlin, from *The Romance of King Arthur and his Knights of the Round Table*, abridged from Sir Thomas Malory's 15th-century Middle English text *Le Morte D'Arthur* by Alfred W. Pollard, and illustrated by Arthur Rackham. Published in New York by Macmillan in 1920; **Right:** Engraving by Richard Westall RA, from the poem *The Lady of the Lake* by Sir Walter Scott, first published in 1810; **Top, right:** A digitally-generated modern fantasy illustration of the Lady of the Lake, from Old World Gods

THE POWER AND MAGIC OF MERLIN

Merlin's birth and early life are shrouded in both magic and prophecy, establishing him as a figure of immense power and wisdom even before his involvement with King Arthur.

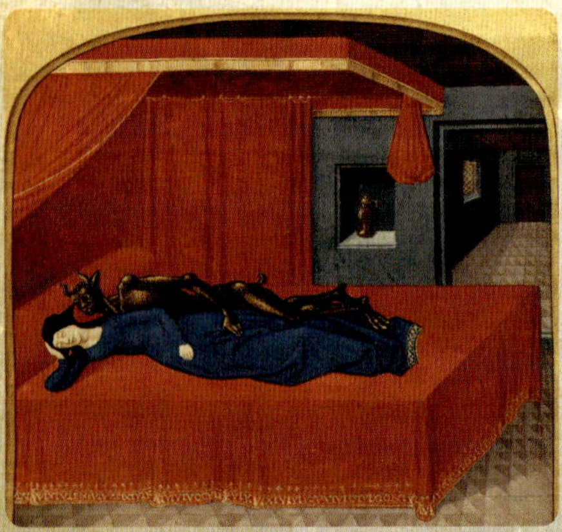

Above: A 15th-century parchment illumination depicting the conception of Merlin: a pure woman of high moral standing, and the "demonic spirit" who put her with child, giving the boy eternal wisdom...and supernatural gifts

Merlin's story is tied to the ancient and often conflicting traditions of Celtic and Christian mythology. According to the most popular version of the tale, Merlin was the son of a mortal woman and an incubus, a demonic spirit. His mother, a devout Christian woman of noble birth, lived in a small village in Wales. The stories vary, but most agree that she was either a nun or a woman of high moral standing who had taken a vow of chastity. Despite her virtuous life, she was visited by a demonic spirit in the night, who seduced her and left her with child. When the woman discovered she was pregnant, she was horrified, fearing the social and religious consequences of bearing a child out of wedlock, especially one fathered by a demon. She sought counsel from a local priest or bishop, who, upon learning of the supernatural circumstances, decided that the child must be baptized and dedicated to God immediately after birth to protect him from the influence of his demonic father. Merlin was born under these dire circumstances, with many fearing that the child would be a monstrous being or possessed by evil. However, the baptism seemed to purify him, and instead of being a creature of darkness, Merlin was born with extraordinary gifts. From a young age, he displayed powers of prophecy, clairvoyance, and magic, abilities that set him apart from other children. His mother, despite her initial fears, raised Merlin with love and care, and she tried to protect him from those who might seek to harm or exploit him.

Merlin's early childhood was marked by a series of miraculous events that showcased his burgeoning powers. One such story tells of a time when Merlin, still a young boy, was brought before the tyrannical King Vortigern, who ruled Britain before Uther Pendragon. Vortigern, facing rebellion and external threats, sought to build an impregnable fortress. However, every time his men tried to lay the foundation, the ground would swallow the stones, making construction impossible.

The king's advisors suggested that the blood of a fatherless child could stabilize the ground and allow the fortress to be built. Merlin, as the son of a demon and a mortal woman, was identified as such a child, and he was brought before the king to be sacrificed. However, when Merlin stood before Vortigern, he revealed his true nature and prophesied the real reason for the collapsing foundation.

Merlin explained that two dragons lay beneath the earth—one red and one white—locked in eternal combat. Their struggle caused the ground to be unstable, and it was this battle, not a lack of sacrifice, that prevented the fortress from being built. Vortigern, intrigued by the boy's wisdom, ordered his men to dig into the earth. To everyone's astonishment, they uncovered the two dragons just as Merlin had foretold. The dragons emerged from the ground, continuing their fierce battle until the red dragon finally triumphed, symbolizing the coming victory of the Britons over their Saxon enemies, as Merlin prophesied. This event marked the beginning of Merlin's reputation as a powerful seer and mage.

Vortigern, recognizing Merlin's unique abilities, spared his life and sought to use his powers for his own gain. However, Merlin, even as a child, was not one to be easily manipulated. He used his gifts wisely, often aiding those who were just and deserving while thwarting the plans of those who sought power for selfish reasons.

As Merlin grew older, his powers only became stronger as he continued to develop his skills in magic, prophecy, and alchemy. His dual heritage—part human, part supernatural—allowed him to bridge the gap between the mortal world and the mystical realms. As Merlin matured, he became more than just a sorcerer or prophet; he became a mentor, a guide, and a protector of the future King Arthur.

Top: The illumination of an English 15th-century manuscript page of *Historia Regum Britanniae*, showing King Vortigern, the tyrannical King of the Britons, witnessing the struggle between the red and white dragons, an event which, after the departure of the Romans from Britain in 409 AD, was purported to signify the coming victory of the Celtic Britons over the invading European Saxons—as Merlin had prophesied; **Above:** One of the many similar portrayals of Merlin, circa early 19th-century; **Opposite top:** In yet another re-writing of the myth of Arthur, Jude Law stars as Vortigern—Uther Pendragon's "usurper brother," in *King Arthur: Legend of the Sword*, Warner's 2017 movie, directed by Guy Ritchie

THE BIRTH OF ARTHUR

In the time of the legendary King Uther Pendragon, Britain was in turmoil, threatened by internal strife and external enemies.

Above: Uther and Igraine, by W Benda, the Polish-American artist, 1903; **Top:** Merlin and the infant Arthur, a modern fantasy work by IonicAI on DeviantArt

Uther, the reigning king, was a powerful but troubled ruler, beset by desires that would shape the destiny of the kingdom. The tale of Arthur's birth begins with Uther's intense longing for Igraine, the wife of the Duke of Cornwall, Gorlois.

Igraine was renowned for her beauty, and Uther's desire for her led him to wage war against Gorlois, attempting to take by force what he could not have by right. As the conflict between Uther and Gorlois raged, Merlin, a wise and enigmatic sorcerer, offered Uther a solution to his predicament. Merlin agreed to help Uther win Igraine, but in return, he demanded that any child born from the union would be given to him for upbringing. Desperate and blinded by his passion, Uther agreed to the bargain.

Merlin used his magical powers to transform Uther's appearance into that of Gorlois, thus allowing him to enter Tintagel, the stronghold where Igraine resided, undetected. Believing Uther to be her husband, Igraine welcomed him into her bed, and that night, Arthur was conceived.

Meanwhile, Gorlois was killed in battle, and the news of his death reached Igraine shortly after. Distraught, she was soon visited by Uther, who revealed his true identity and his actions. Despite the deception, Uther married Igraine, and she became the queen of Britain.

When Arthur was born, Uther kept his promise to Merlin and handed the child over to the wizard. Merlin, knowing the dangers that lay ahead, decided to place

the infant in the care of Sir Ector, a loyal and noble knight who lived far from the court's intrigues. Sir Ector raised Arthur as his own son, alongside his biological son, Sir Kay, without revealing his true lineage. Arthur grew up unaware of his royal blood, living a humble life under Sir Ector's guidance, where he learned the values of chivalry, honor, and humility.

During Arthur's childhood, Uther continued to rule, but his reign was marked by increasing unrest. The king fell ill and, sensing his death was near, sought Merlin's counsel. Merlin warned Uther that Britain would descend into chaos after his death unless a rightful king could be identified. On his deathbed, Uther revealed to his most trusted advisors the secret of Arthur's birth and his rightful claim to the throne. Shortly after this proclamation, Uther died, and the kingdom plunged into a period of anarchy, with various lords and nobles vying for power.

The identity of the true heir remained hidden, with Arthur growing up in obscurity. His destiny, however, was sealed, as Merlin's plan to reveal the future king was set into motion.

Above: *Merlin Presenting the Future King Arthur*, by Emil Johann Lauffer, 1878. Harking back to his pre-Christian Celtic origins, Merlin is often linked to stags, and has an association with the horned deity Cernunnos; **Below:** *The Infant Arthur Taken by Merlin*, book illustration, circa 1950s

THE SWORD IN THE STONE

In the aftermath of King Uther Pendragon's death, with no clear heir to the throne, Britain fell into chaos.

The kingdom was on the brink of civil war, the people of Britain suffered under constant strife, and it seemed that the land would never know peace again.

Amidst this turmoil, Merlin, the wise and mysterious sorcerer who had been Uther's advisor, devised a plan to reveal the true king. Merlin knew that Arthur, Uther's secret son, was destined to unite Britain, but the boy was still unknown to the world, living quietly as the foster son of Sir Ector, a loyal knight. To bring Arthur's destiny to light, Merlin arranged for a miraculous event that would be witnessed by all.

On Christmas Eve, a great assembly was called, where nobles, knights, and commoners alike gathered for a grand tournament. At the heart of the event was an extraordinary sight: a massive stone with an anvil atop it, and embedded in the anvil was a gleaming sword. This sword bore an inscription that read: "Whoso pulleth out this sword of this stone and anvil is rightwise king born of all England." The sword was none other than Excalibur, a weapon of mystical origin, bound to the true king.

News of this challenge spread quickly, and many men, both noble and common, attempted to pull the sword from the stone, but all failed. The stone and sword remained firmly in place, immovable by even the strongest or most cunning warriors. The people began to believe that the sword would remain in the stone forever, and the rightful king would never be found.

Arthur, at this time, was still a young boy, unaware of his royal heritage. He had come to the tournament not as a participant but as a squire to his foster brother, Sir Kay. Arthur's role was simple: to assist Sir Kay, tending to his armor, weapons, and ensuring everything was in place for the competition. On the morning of the tournament, in the hustle and bustle of preparations, Sir Kay realized he had forgotten his sword. Desperate to retrieve

Above: There are several "swords in the stone" dotted around Wales, the West Country of England, France, and other ancient Celtic locations in Europe, even Italy (see over). This one is at Taunton Castle in Somerset; **Opposite:** A young Arthur effortlessly succeeds in drawing the sword from its stone in this illustration from Henrietta Elizabeth Marshall's book *Our Island Story*, of 1906. Here, as in many more recent depictions of this well-known scene, there is no anvil.

Top, and **Above:** two illustrations of the sword in the stone legend. Both are probably by U.S. artist Howard Pyle, who wrote and illustrated several Arthurian legend novels in the last decade of his life: *The Story of King Arthur and His Knights*, 1903; *The Story of the Champions of the Round Table*, 1905; *The Story of Sir Launcelot and His Companions*, 1907; and *The Story of the Grail and the Passing of King Arthur*, 1910; **Main image, above right:** Llangorse Lake in the Brecon Beacons region of Powys, Wales, with its sword in the stone in the foreground.

it before his match, he sent Arthur back to their lodging to fetch it.

Arthur hurried back to the house but found it locked and the sword inaccessible. Not wanting to disappoint Sir Kay, Arthur searched for an alternative. As he wandered the streets, he came upon the churchyard where the sword in the stone stood, seemingly forgotten in the excitement of the tournament. Without thinking much of it, Arthur approached the sword. To him, it seemed a simple solution to his problem; he needed a sword, and here was one freely available. Arthur grasped the hilt of the sword, and to his surprise, it slid effortlessly from the stone. He marveled at how easily it came free, not knowing the significance of his action. With the sword in hand, he ran back to Sir Kay, presenting it to him. Sir Kay immediately recognized the sword and was stunned. He quickly realized that his young brother had unwittingly achieved what no other knight could.

Kay brought the sword to his father, Sir Ector, who was equally astonished. Realizing the gravity of the situation, Sir Ector took Arthur and Sir Kay back to the churchyard where the stone stood. Sir Ector asked Arthur to replace the sword into the stone, and the boy did so without difficulty.

THE CELTIC WORLD
The Italian Sword in the Stone

Montesiepi Chapel, Tuscany, Italy (above and right), and its sword in the stone (above right). The chapel stands on the hill where the 12th-century knight Galgano Guidotti (later Saint Galgano) plunged his sword into a rock and began his life as a Hermit. Down the hill is the ruined Abbey of San Galgano.

Then, at Sir Ector's request, Arthur drew the sword out once more with ease. At that moment, Sir Ector and Sir Kay knelt before Arthur, recognizing him as the rightful king of Britain.

Arthur, bewildered by their actions, protested, saying he was not a king, just a simple squire. But Sir Ector revealed to Arthur his true lineage, explaining that he was the son of Uther Pendragon, placed in Sir Ector's care by Merlin for his protection. Arthur was shocked and overwhelmed, struggling to comprehend his new identity and the responsibilities that came with it. News of Arthur's feat quickly spread throughout the kingdom, and the other nobles demanded to witness the miracle for themselves. Another assembly was called, where many of the greatest lords and knights in Britain gathered to see if the boy could truly draw the sword from the stone.

Arthur performed the feat again in front of all assembled, and despite their initial reluctance to accept a boy as their king, the nobles eventually acknowledged Arthur as the rightful ruler, for none could deny the divine will that had guided his hand.

Inset, above left: Montesiepi Chapel, Tuscany, Italy, and **(top right)** its sword in the stone; **Above right:** The chapel is built around its sword in the stone, and stands on the hill where the 12th-century knight Galgano Guidotti, later Saint Galgano, plunged his sword into a rock and began his life as a Hermit. Down the hill is the ruined Abbey of San Galgano.

THE ORIGIN OF LANCELOT

Lancelot, one of the greatest knights of the Round Table, began his life far from the courts of Camelot, in a world shrouded in mystery and magic.

Lancelot's origins are rooted in both tragedy and destiny, setting the stage for the heroic yet tumultuous life he would lead.

Lancelot was born to King Ban of Benoic and Queen Elaine, rulers of a small but noble kingdom in what is now modern-day France. Ban was a loyal ally of King Arthur, fighting alongside him to secure the lands of Britain. However, Ban's kingdom was under constant threat from the treacherous King Claudas, a powerful and ruthless rival who sought to expand his dominion by any means necessary.

When Lancelot was just an infant, Claudas launched a devastating attack on Benoic, forcing King Ban and his queen to flee with their son. Ban, desperate to protect his family, fought valiantly to defend his castle, but his forces were overwhelmed. As Ban lay mortally wounded, Queen Elaine fled into the woods with the infant Lancelot, her heart heavy with grief and fear.

Amidst the chaos, Elaine sought refuge near a lake, where she was met by a mysterious and ethereal figure—the Lady of the Lake, a powerful enchantress who dwelled in the magical waters. The Lady of the Lake had been watching over the child, knowing that he was destined for greatness. She offered to take Lancelot into her care, promising to protect him from the dangers of the world and to raise him in her mystical realm. With a heavy heart, Elaine agreed, knowing that this was the only way to ensure her son's safety.

The Lady of the Lake took the infant Lancelot into her arms and carried him to

her enchanted home beneath the waters. There, Lancelot grew up in a world of magic, far removed from the turmoil of his birthright. He was nurtured by the Lady, who became both a mother figure and a mentor, teaching him the ways of chivalry, honor, and combat.

As Lancelot matured, he became a formidable warrior, his skills unmatched by any other knight. The Lady of the Lake, recognizing that Lancelot was ready to fulfill his destiny, revealed to him his true heritage—that he was the son of King Ban and a prince of Benoic. She also told him of his duty to join King Arthur's court and become a knight of the Round Table, where he would play a crucial role in the defense of the realm.

Lancelot, armed with the knowledge of his lineage and the skills he had honed under the Lady's tutelage, left the enchanted lake to seek out King Arthur. Upon arriving at Camelot, Lancelot's prowess and noble bearing quickly earned him a place among the greatest knights of the kingdom. He became Arthur's closest friend and most trusted champion, known for his bravery, loyalty, and unmatched skill in battle.

Above: *Lancelot and Guinevere* by the Scottish painter James Archer, circa 1860; **Left:** Lancelot slays the dragon of Corbenic in Arthur Rackham's illustration for *Tales of King Arthur and the Knights of the Round Table*, by Alfred W. Pollard, 1917, and abridged from *Le Morte d'Arthur*; **Main image, top:** *Lancelot Brings Guinevere to Arthur*, from *The Book of Romance*, Andrew Lang, 1902; **Opposite, top right:** The faery enchantress Nimue, the Lady of the Lake, bears away the infant Lancelot and gives him a magical upbringing. From *The Story of the Champions of the Round Table*, by Howard Pyle, 1905; **Opposite, bottom left:** *Lancelot in armour*, by Eleanor Fortesque-Brickdale, part of her commission for an edition of Tennyson's *Idylls of the King*, published in 1911. The 28 pictures were completed from 1909-1911 and exhibited in 1911.

MORDRED

Morgause was Arthur's half-sister, though neither of them knew this at the time. She was the daughter of Igraine and Gorlois, making her a sibling to Arthur by blood...

Above: Joan Allen plays Morgause, Arthur's half-sister, with Hans Matheson playing their incestuously conceived son Mordred, in the 2001 movie *The Mists of Avalon*. Copyright Warner Bros/ Cinematic Collection; **Top:** "How Mordred was slain by Arthur, and how by him Arthur was hurt to the death..." from the Book *The Romance of King Arthur and his Knights of the Round Table*, abridged by Alfred W. Pollard from Sir Thomas Malory's *Morte d'Arthur*. Illustrated by Arthur Rackham and published by Macmillan in New York, 1920.

During one of his early campaigns, Arthur visited Morgause's court, where he was struck by her beauty and charm. Unaware of their familial connection, Arthur and Morgause shared a night together, a union that was both unplanned and ill-fated.

From this encounter, Morgause conceived a child—Mordred. While Arthur returned to his kingdom, Morgause carried the child in secret. When Mordred was born, he was raised at the court of King Lot, alongside his brothers Gawain, Agravain, Gaheris, and Gareth, who would later become knights of the Round Table. Mordred, however, was different from his brothers, marked by the circumstances of his conception and the dark prophecy that surrounded his birth.

Prophecy played a significant role in the life of Arthur and his kingdom. Merlin, the wise and powerful wizard who served as Arthur's advisor, had foreseen the coming of Mordred and the destruction he would bring. According to the prophecy, Arthur was warned that a child born on May Day—his own offspring—would one day rise against him and lead to the ruin of Camelot.

In a desperate attempt to prevent this prophecy from coming true, Arthur ordered that all noble children born on May Day be gathered and sent away in a ship, hoping to eliminate the threat. The ship, carrying the innocent children, was set adrift at sea, intended to meet a tragic end. However, fate intervened, and the ship was wrecked upon the rocky shores. Though many

children perished, Mordred survived and was eventually rescued, unbeknownst to Arthur.

Mordred was brought back to the court of King Lot, where he was raised, still ignorant of his true lineage. As he grew, Mordred became aware of the dark prophecy that surrounded his birth. The knowledge of his true parentage—being both Arthur's son and nephew—festered within him, fueling a deep resentment and a desire for power.

Mordred's destiny would intertwine with Arthur's once more when he came of age and joined the court of Camelot. Though he was welcomed as a knight of the Round Table, his presence was a harbinger of the doom that was foretold. The birth of Mordred set in motion the tragic events that would eventually lead to the fall of Camelot, fulfilling the prophecy that had loomed over Arthur's life since the beginning.

Above: A depiction of the fateful battle Between King Arthur and Mordred—Arthur runs Mordred through with his lance, or spear, but Mordred deals Arthur a fatal blow as he dies. A work by the English illustrator William Hatherell, circa 1910; **Top:** Christopher Bowen as Mordred, with Jean Marsh as Morgaine (*aka* Morgan Le Fay, and in some variations of the myth, sister of Morgause, the mother of Mordred), on location in May 1989, filming the BBC Doctor Who story *Battlefield*

EXCALIBUR

The sword Excalibur is one of the most significant objects in Arthurian legend, symbolizing the divine kingship, authority, and the rightful sovereignty of King Arthur.

Above: King Arthur, with Merlin in the background, sees the sword Excalibur held aloft from within the lake. The origin of the Lady in the Lake myth could be traced back to the votive offerings of the Celts, which were frequently submerged in lakes. The illustration, from 1923, is probably by Louis Rhead, taken from Sir James Knowles's *The Story of King Arthur & His Knights.*

Excalibur is imbued with mystical qualities and is associated with several key moments in the mythos surrounding Arthur's reign.

Origins and Acquisition

Excalibur's origins vary across different versions of Arthurian tales. In one popular account, Excalibur is the sword that Arthur pulls from the stone, an act that proves his divine right to rule as King of Britain. This version of the story emphasizes the sword's role as a symbol of legitimate kingship. The act of drawing the sword from the stone demonstrates Arthur's worthiness and destiny, marking him as the chosen one by divine will.

In another version of the myth, Excalibur is given to Arthur by the Lady of the Lake, a mysterious and powerful enchantress who resides in a mystical body of water. According to this account, Arthur already possesses the sword he pulled from the stone, but Excalibur, bestowed by the Lady of the Lake, is a separate and more powerful weapon. The sword is retrieved from beneath the waters, emphasizing its otherworldly origin and the magical protection it offers to the king. The Lady of the Lake's role in this version highlights the connection between Arthur and the supernatural forces that guide and protect his reign.

Magical Properties

Excalibur is often described as a sword of unparalleled quality, unmatched by any other weapon. It is said to be unbreakable and to have a blade that shines as bright as the sun, blinding Arthur's enemies in battle. The sword's scabbard is also of great importance, often considered even more valuable than the sword itself. According

to legend, while Arthur possesses the scabbard, he cannot be mortally wounded. This aspect of the myth underscores the idea that Excalibur is not just a weapon of war but a protective talisman that ensures the survival and success of the true king.

Symbolism

Excalibur's symbolism extends beyond its physical attributes. The sword represents the divine right of kingship, chosen by higher powers to rule with justice and wisdom. It is also a symbol of Arthur's connection to the mystical and magical elements of the world, which play a crucial role in the establishment and maintenance of his kingdom. The sword's association with both the stone and the lake connects it to the earth and water, grounding Arthur's kingship in the natural and supernatural realms. The loss of Excalibur is equally significant. According to the legend, as Arthur lay dying after the Battle of Camlann, he ordered Sir Bedivere to return Excalibur to the Lady of the Lake. After two initial hesitations, Bedivere finally casts the sword back into the lake, where a hand emerges, catches the sword, and draws it back beneath the surface. This act symbolizes the end of Arthur's reign—and the passing of his legacy back to the mystical forces that had first granted him power over Camelot and the kingdom.

Top, main image: With pictures painted by Edmund Dulac, the French-British illustrator, *The Tale of Arthur's Sword Excalibur* was one of a series of articles on Arthurian Legend that were published in *The American Weekly* Sunday magazine during 1940; **Above right:** After the death of Arthur, Sir Bedivere returns Excalibur back to the mystical prophet and sorcerer Nimue, the Lady of the Lake

The Knights of the Round Table hold a central place in Arthurian legend, symbolizing the highest ideals of chivalry, loyalty, and martial prowess.

Top, left: *Sir Galahad, during his Quest for the Holy Grail*. Painted by Arthur Hughes, circa late 19th-century; **Top, right:** Emblem of the Knights of The Round Table in the medieval Great Hall of Winchester Castle, England; **Above:** *Sir Galahad fights the Knights of Darkness*, 1902

The Round Table itself is a powerful symbol of equality, with its circular shape ensuring that no knight, not even King Arthur, sits at its head. The concept of the Round Table first appears in the work of the Norman poet Wace in his *Roman de Brut* of 1155, which expanded on earlier legends.

This innovation became a cornerstone of the Arthurian mythos, representing a utopian vision of chivalric brotherhood. Malory's *Le Morte d'Arthur* (1485) is one of the most comprehensive accounts of the knights' exploits, weaving together various strands of Arthurian legend into a single, cohesive narrative.

The Code of Chivalry

Membership in the Round Table was reserved for those knights who exemplified the chivalric virtues of honor, courage, loyalty, and piety. These knights were bound by a strict code of conduct, which dictated their behavior both in battle and in their personal lives. The code emphasized the protection of the weak and innocent, the defense of the realm, and the pursuit of justice. It also included a strong spiritual dimension, particularly in the later romances where quests for holy relics, such as the Holy Grail, became paramount. The Round Table thus represented not only martial excellence but also moral and spiritual integrity.

KNIGHTS OF THE ROUND TABLE

Notable Knights

The legends of the Round Table feature a vast array of knights, each with their own stories and virtues. Among them, a few stand out for their prominence and the roles they play in the most famous Arthurian tales:

Sir Lancelot: Renowned for his unmatched skills in combat, he is one of the most celebrated knights of the Round Table. His deep—and ultimately destructive—love for Queen Guinevere creates a tragic tension within the Arthurian court. Lancelot's story is one of both glory and downfall, as his affair with the queen leads to the eventual collapse of the Round Table.

Sir Gawain: Often depicted as the epitome of knightly virtue, Sir Gawain is known for his unwavering loyalty to King Arthur. His moral fortitude is famously tested in the tale of Sir Gawain and the Green Knight, where he confronts both supernatural and ethical challenges that explore the complexities of the chivalric code.

Sir Galahad: The son of Lancelot and Elaine, Sir Galahad is portrayed as the most spiritually pure of all the knights. His purity allows him to succeed in the quest for the Holy Grail, a quest that is central to the later Arthurian romances. Galahad's character embodies the spiritual ideals of knighthood, representing the quest for divine perfection.

Sir Percival: Another key figure in the Grail quest, Sir Percival is often depicted as a naive young knight whose innocence and simplicity lead him toward spiritual enlightenment. In some versions of the legend, Percival achieves the Grail, although this role is sometimes shared or replaced by Galahad.

Top, left: In the Arthurian myths, the Round Table knights experienced visions of The Grail during their quests. English, circa late 19th-century; **Top, right:** *The Admission of Sir Tristram to the Round Table*, engraving, circa late 18th-century; **Above:** *I am Sir Launcelot du Lake, and Knight of the Round Table*. The meeting between Lancelot and Sir Turquine, from *The Boy's King Arthur*, by Sidney Lanie, 1917. The painting is by Newell Convers Wyeth.

Despite his wisdom, Merlin was not immune to the emotions and weaknesses that plague all humans. His encounter with Viviane, a young and beautiful enchantress, would ultimately lead to his downfall.

MERLIN AND VIVIANE

Merlin, the great wizard and advisor to King Arthur, was known for his immense knowledge, magical prowess, and foresight, and the tale begins with Merlin encountering Viviane, often described as a young woman of extraordinary beauty and charm, near a mystical body of water—a lake or a forest spring.

Viviane, aware of Merlin's power and reputation, sought to learn the secrets of his magic. Different versions of the myth provide varying motives for Viviane's actions—some suggest she was ambitious and desired power, while others imply that she was a servant of higher, mysterious forces.

Merlin, captivated by Viviane's beauty and charm, fell deeply in love with her despite his awareness of the potential dangers. His affection for Viviane was so great that he agreed to teach her all the secrets of his magic. As their relationship grew, Merlin became increasingly infatuated, blinded by his emotions, and less wary of the consequences. Viviane, however, was more pragmatic. She understood the importance of the power Merlin wielded and sought to protect herself from him, should his love ever turn to anger or jealousy. Merlin, in his love-struck state, shared with Viviane all his knowledge, including powerful spells of entrapment. Viviane, though seemingly innocent, harbored a plan to use this knowledge against Merlin. She feared his power and believed that the only way to secure her safety was to bind Merlin in such a way that he could never harm her or control her.

In a secluded place, often described as an enchanted forest or a cave, Viviane used the very magic that Merlin had taught her. Depending on which version of the story read, she cast a spell of entrapment, binding Merlin within a tree, a crystal cave, or some other mystical prison. The spell is so potent that even Merlin, with all his power and foresight, could not escape. He is trapped for eternity, unable to help or advise King Arthur or influence the events that are soon to unfold.

Merlin's imprisonment marks a turning point in Arthurian legend. Without Merlin's guidance, Arthur and his knights face increasing challenges which ultimately lead to the eventual downfall of Camelot. Some versions of the myth suggest that Viviane acted not out of malice, but rather from a desire to prevent the mighty wizard from interfering with the future she had seen.

Above: Merlin and Viviane, by Albert Herter, from *Tales of the Enchanted Islands of the Atlantic*, by TW Higginson, 1899; **Opposite:** *Merlin and Viviane in the Forest*, hand-colored woodcut by the prolific French engraver Gustave Doré, circa 1880s

MORGAN LE FAY AND ACCOLON

Morgan Le Fay, King Arthur's half-sister, was a powerful sorceress with ambitions that put her at odds with the king.

Above: Morgan Le Fay and Sir Accolon of Gaul. In *Le Morte d'Arthur* Accolon is a knight of the Round Table, and is both the object of her desire and the means by which she hoped to take control of the kingdom. She uses Accolon in her plan to kill Arthur and seize the throne. Picture by any_s_kill at DeviantArt.

Despite her familial ties, Morgan harbored deep resentment toward Arthur, largely due to his rejection of her magical practices and her desire for power. Over time, her bitterness grew, and she plotted to overthrow Arthur and claim the throne for herself.

Morgan's most daring plan involved her lover, Sir Accolon of Gaul, a knight loyal to her above all others. She sought to use Accolon as a pawn in her scheme to defeat Arthur and seize power. Through her magical abilities, Morgan crafted a detailed and dangerous plot to trap Arthur and ensure that Accolon would kill him in combat.

One day, while Arthur and his knights were out hunting, they became separated, and Arthur found himself lost in a dense forest. As night fell, he stumbled upon a mysterious and beautiful pavilion. Exhausted, Arthur entered the tent and found a bed where he could rest. As he slept, Morgan's enchantments took hold. She transported Arthur to an unfamiliar and enchanted castle, while also manipulating Accolon into a similar situation. Accolon, unaware of Morgan's full plan but eager to serve her, awoke in a different part of the same castle, where Morgan appeared to him in a vision. She handed him the magical sword Excalibur, which she had stolen from Arthur, and instructed him to use it to defeat a mysterious opponent who would challenge him. Accolon, trusting Morgan completely, vowed to do as she asked.

The following day, Arthur and Accolon were brought together in the castle's courtyard, each unaware of the other's identity due to the enchantments placed upon them. They were told by the castle's lord that they must fight to the death. Accolon, armed with Excalibur, was confident in his victory, while Arthur was given a counterfeit sword, making him vulnerable.

The battle began, and Accolon quickly gained the upper hand. With each strike, Arthur grew weaker, unable to match the power of Excalibur. Despite his wounds, Arthur fought valiantly, but it seemed inevitable that Accolon would prevail.

However, fate intervened. The Lady of the Lake, who had originally given Excalibur to Arthur, sensed the theft of the sword and the danger Arthur was in. She appeared at the castle, using her own magic to weaken Morgan's enchantments. As Arthur struggled to stay alive, he suddenly realized

that the sword he held was a fake, and his opponent was wielding Excalibur.

In a moment of clarity, Arthur summoned all his strength and managed to disarm Accolon. With Excalibur back in his hand, the tide of the battle turned. Arthur wounded Accolon severely, but before he could deliver the final blow, Accolon recognized his king and realized the full extent of Morgan's betrayal. He confessed everything to Arthur, revealing Morgan's treachery.

Arthur spared Accolon's life but was deeply troubled by Morgan's actions. He ordered that Accolon be cared for, but the knight soon died from his wounds. Arthur confronted Morgan, who fled before she could be captured. Though she escaped, her plot had failed, and Arthur's trust in his sister was shattered forever.

Main image above left: Morgan Le Fay and Accolon, her bewitched lover, engraved print, George Frederic Watts RA. English, circa 1860; **Top:** After her enchantments took hold on both King Arthur and Accolon, Morgan steals into Arthur's room and takes Excalibur in its scabbard. Pen and ink, early 20th-century; **Above:** Sir Accolon, wielding Excalibur, gets the better of King Arthur, in Eric Pape's illustration for Madison Cawein's poem *Accolon of Gaul*, from 1907

THE QUEST FOR THE HOLY GRAIL

The quest for the Holy Grail began in the court of King Arthur when a mysterious vision appeared to the knights of the Round Table during a feast.

The Grail, a sacred relic believed to be the cup used by Jesus Christ at the Last Supper, was seen briefly, veiled in light, and accompanied by a sense of divine presence. This vision filled the hearts of the knights with a holy fervor, and many of them vowed to set out on a quest to find the Grail, believing that it would bring salvation to their souls and restore the kingdom to its former glory.

The most prominent knights who embarked on this quest were Sir Galahad, Sir Lancelot, Sir Percival, and Sir Bors. Each knight's journey was marked by trials that tested their faith, purity, and adherence to the chivalric code.

Sir Galahad, the son of Sir Lancelot, was the purest of all the knights. He had been raised by nuns and trained in the ways of chivalry and spirituality, and from a young age, it was clear that he was destined for greatness. Galahad's purity was such that he was chosen to sit in the *Siege Perilous*, a seat at the Round Table reserved for the knight who would find the Grail. Anyone unworthy who sat in this seat would be struck dead, but Galahad sat safely, confirming his role in the quest. His journey was one of divine guidance. He encountered many challenges, but each time, his unwavering faith and purity allowed him to overcome them. In one instance, Galahad arrived at a castle where a crippled king lay suffering from a grievous wound.

This was the Fisher King, who had been wounded and left in a state of perpetual agony due to a sin committed by someone in his line. The Grail was the only thing that could heal him, and Galahad, through his prayer and devotion, received a vision that guided him to the Grail's location.

Meanwhile, Sir Lancelot, who was widely regarded as the greatest knight in terms of martial prowess, struggled with his own demons during the quest. Though he was brave and noble, Lancelot was haunted by his love for Queen Guinevere, which was a source of great shame and guilt for him. His adulterous relationship with the queen tainted his soul, preventing him from achieving the spiritual purity required to find the Grail. At one point in his journey, Lancelot reached a castle where the Grail

Opposite: At the Castle of Corbin, a shimmering maiden appears, offering a vision of the *Sangreal*—the Holy Grail—and foretelling of the achievements of Sir Galahad; **Above:** In this 15th-century parchment illumination, the Knights of the Round Table behold the revelation of the Holy Grail, filling the knights with a holy fervor to seek out the cup of Christ

Top: *The Temptation of Sir Percival* by Arthur Hacker, 1894; **Above:** The Grail appears to Sir Galahad. Woodcut by WJ Enright, December 1923

was kept, but as he approached it, he was struck down and rendered unconscious, forbidden from entering due to his sins. Sir Percival, another key figure in the quest, was a knight known for his innocence and simplicity. His journey was marked by encounters with various temptations and illusions, designed to lead him astray. In one of his trials, Percival met a beautiful woman who offered him her love and the comforts of a luxurious life. Though tempted, Percival resisted, realizing that these were distractions from his holy mission. He continued his quest, driven by a deep sense of duty and the hope of achieving spiritual fulfillment.

Sir Bors, the cousin of Lancelot, also faced severe trials during his quest. Unlike the other knights, Bors was a more practical man, often caught between his duties as a knight and his responsibilities as a family man. His greatest test came when he was forced to choose between saving his brother Lionel, who was in mortal danger, and rescuing a maiden in distress. Torn by the decision, Bors chose to save the maiden, believing it was the more virtuous act, and prayed for his brother's safety. By divine intervention, both his brother and the maiden were saved, and Bors continued his journey with a clear conscience.

As the quest progressed, many knights fell away, either succumbing to temptations or meeting untimely deaths. The journey to find the Grail was a spiritual trial as much as it was a physical one, and only those of the purest heart could hope to succeed. Eventually, Sir Galahad, accompanied by Sir Percival and Sir Bors, arrived at the mystical city of Sarras, where the Grail was kept. The city was filled with wonders and challenges that tested their faith, but Galahad, through his pure heart and divine favor, was able to withstand all trials. Upon entering the chamber where the Grail was housed, Galahad was filled

THE CELTIC WORLD
Richard Wagner's *Parsifal*

Richard Wagner's libretto for his music drama *Parsifal* draws on two early medieval chivalric romances: the Old French *Perceval ou le Conte du Graal* by the 12th-century trouvère Chrétien de Troyes, and the 13th-century German *Parzival of the Minnesänger* by Eschenbach. Both recount versions of the Arthurian knight Sir Percival and his spiritual journey for the Holy Grail.

with a divine light, and he knelt before the sacred relic. In that moment, he prayed for the grace to pass from this world, having achieved his earthly mission.

His prayer was answered, and Galahad's soul was taken to heaven, leaving behind his mortal body. Sir Percival and Sir Bors, awed by what they had witnessed, remained in Sarras for a time. Percival, deeply moved by Galahad's spiritual journey, chose to live a life of asceticism and eventually passed away in the city, content with his life's purpose fulfilled.

Sir Bors, the only knight to return to Camelot, brought the news of the quest's completion and the fate of his companions. He recounted the divine experiences and the ultimate success of Sir Galahad in finding the Grail. However, despite this triumph, the quest had a somber effect on Camelot. Many knights had perished, and the fellowship of the Round Table was fractured.

The quest for the Holy Grail, while a story of spiritual achievement and divine favor, also marked the beginning of the decline of Arthur's kingdom. The loss of so many knights and the strain on the remaining ones weakened the unity of the Round Table, setting the stage for the eventual downfall of Camelot. Nonetheless, the tale of the Grail quest remains one of the most profound and enduring stories of Arthurian legend, symbolizing the eternal human quest for divine grace and spiritual fulfillment.

Inset, above right: A scene from *Parsifal*, Richard Wagner's music drama opera. His libretto for the work draws on two early medieval chivalric romances: the Old French *Perceval ou le Conte du Graal* by the 12th-century trouvère Chrétien de Troyes, and the 13th-century German *Parzival of the Minnesänger* by Eschenbach. Both recount versions of the Arthurian knight Sir Percival and his spiritual journey for the Holy Grail. Drawn by Emil Doepler the Younger; **Inset, above left:** Another scene from *Parsifal*, "the washing of the feet," also by Emil Doepler, late 19th-century wood engraving

THE CELTIC WORLD
Le Tombeau de Merlin
Forest of Paimpont

The Tombeau de Merlin—Merlin's Tomb—is a megalithic monument dating from the Neolithic period located in the Forest of Paimpont, at a place called La Marette near the hamlet of Landelles in Paimpont. A medieval tradition passed down told that Merlin's tomb was in the legendary forest of Brocéliande, and famed archaeologist Félix Bellamy definined its location in 1889.

Shortly afterward the Tombeau de Merlin was largely destroyed by grave robbers, but it has nevertheless become an important tourist site. In Britain, Bardsey Island in Wales, and Drumelzier, in the Tweed Valley of the Scottish Borders, also claim to have Merlin's grave.

The Tombeau de Merlin at La Marette is a megalithic construction dating from the Neolithic era, of the gallery grave type. According to Félix Bellamy there were originally two gallery graves; of these one, already in ruins, called the *Tombeau de Merlin* (the second was designated as the Tomb of Viviane) was the subject of a detailed description in the 1920s.

It was 34 ft long and 4.9 ft wide. The room was delimited by four orthostats on one side, only one on the other and a sixth slab acted as an apse. The height of these supports varied from 3.0 ft to 4.9 ft, the width from 4.1 ft to 5.2 ft and the thickness from 0.82 ft to 1.3 ft. The covering slabs had all collapsed. All the stones of the monument were of *purple schist*. Only three stones are now left. The only known graphic records of the full monument are two 19th-century engravings and an old postcard dated 1900. The Tombeau Merlin is listed on the Base Mérimée, the official French inventory of notable architecture and archaeological monuments.

According to the Lancelot-Grail cycle, Merlin withdrew from the world because of his love for the fairy Viviane, though in another version of the legend, he is imprisoned by Viviane's enchantments in a cave. The poet Auguste Creuzé de Lesser wrote in 1811 that Merlin was buried in the forest of Brocéliande, a legendary forest whose precise location has never really been identified.

The modern history of Merlin's tomb begins in 1820, when a judge and scholar from Montfort-sur-Meu, J. C. D. Poignand, published an article in the Brochure des Antiquités Historiques in which he claimed that Merlin was buried in the Forest of Paimpont, in the commune of Saint-Malon-sur-Mel and near the abbey of Talhouet.

For twenty years the inhabitants searched, hoping to find treasure there. In 1825, the writer Blanchard de la Musse associated a gallery grave in the north of the Forest of Paimpont with the tomb of Merlin. Théodore Hersart de la Villemarqué also located the tomb of Merlin in these places. An 1846 Romantic engraving from the Magasin pittoresque shows a stone circle, non-existent in the Forest of Paimpont, named Tombeau de Merlin and located in the forest of Brocéliande.

The topography of the Forest of Paimpont was defined by Félix Bellamy in 1889. His research, based on Poignand's article and the statements of the inhabitants, led him to settle on this gallery grave as the location of the tomb.

Above: *The Death of King Arthur* by James Archer, 1860. In his death throes Arthur sees a faint vision of The Grail.

In the final days of King Arthur's reign, the once-great kingdom of Camelot was in turmoil, beset by betrayal, internal strife, and the looming shadow of fate. Arthur, who had united the land and established the Round Table, now faced the greatest challenge of his life—one that would lead to his tragic end.

The seeds of Arthur's downfall were sown by the treachery of his nephew, Mordred, who was born of an incestuous union between Arthur and his half-sister, Morgause. Mordred harbored a deep resentment toward Arthur and coveted the throne of Camelot. His opportunity to strike came when Arthur left to wage war against the Roman Emperor Lucius, leaving Mordred in charge of the kingdom. While Arthur was away, Mordred seized power, declaring himself king and attempting to marry Queen Guinevere. Guinevere, loyal to Arthur, fled to the Tower of London and fortified herself

The seeds of Arthur's downfall were sown by the treachery of his incestuous son, Mordred, who was born of a deeply illicit union between Arthur and his half-sister, Morgause...

THE DEATH OF ARTHUR

there. Upon hearing of Mordred's treachery, Arthur quickly returned to Britain, gathering his forces to reclaim his kingdom.

The final confrontation between Arthur and Mordred took place at the Battle of Camlann, a bloody and devastating conflict that would decide the fate of Britain. Both armies met on a field shrouded in mist, as if the very elements mourned the impending tragedy. Before the battle began, Arthur, hoping to avoid unnecessary bloodshed, attempted to negotiate a truce with Mordred. They agreed to meet between their armies, with a small contingent of knights on each side, to discuss terms.

However, both sides were tense and mistrustful. During the parley, a knight on Mordred's side, seeing an adder slither from under a bush, instinctively drew his sword to kill it. This action, misinterpreted as the start of an attack, led to the outbreak of violence. Both armies charged, and the battle erupted into chaos.

The Battle of Camlann was fierce and merciless, with knights and soldiers fighting desperately for their respective causes. Arthur fought valiantly, cutting down many of Mordred's men, but the battle took a heavy toll on both sides. By the end of the day, the battlefield was littered with the bodies of the fallen, including many of Arthur's most loyal knights. Among them was Sir Gawain, Arthur's nephew and one of his greatest warriors, who had been mortally wounded in an earlier skirmish. Before his death, Gawain wrote a letter to Lancelot, begging him to return and aid Arthur, but it was too late.

As the sun began to set, only a few knights remained standing. Arthur, gravely wounded and exhausted, finally faced Mordred in single combat. The two circled each other, each knowing that this battle would end in death. Mordred, consumed by hatred, fought with the ferocity of a man who had nothing to lose. Arthur, despite his injuries, wielded Excalibur with all the strength he could muster.

Above: The mortal battle between Arthur and Sir Mordred—Arthur kills Sir Mordred, but suffers a fatal blow in the process. Painting by William Hatherell, circa 1910

Top: *The Lamentation of King Arthur*, WIlliam Bell Scott, painted over a 15-year period, from 1847 to 1862; **Above:** John Garrick, *The Death of King Arthur*, 1862. Carrick's scene depicts the final moments of Arthur, as Sir Bedivere waits with him for the Barge of the Three Queens

The clash between uncle and nephew was brutal and swift. Arthur struck Mordred with a powerful blow, driving his spear through Mordred's body. But as Mordred felt the life drain from him, he gathered the last of his strength and delivered a final, fatal strike to Arthur's head with his sword. Mordred fell dead at Arthur's feet, but the king, too, had been mortally wounded.

Bleeding and weak, Arthur knew his time was short. He called for his last remaining knights, Sir Bedivere and Sir Lucan, to help him. Lucan, despite his own wounds, tried to lift Arthur, but in the effort, his injuries worsened, and he died at his king's side. Bedivere, the sole survivor, cradled Arthur and listened to his final commands.

Arthur instructed Bedivere to take Excalibur, the legendary sword that had marked his kingship, and return it to the Lady of the Lake from whence it came. Bedivere, unwilling to part with such a precious relic, hesitated. Twice he hid the sword instead of throwing it into the lake, but Arthur, sensing the knight's reluctance, demanded to know what he had seen when he cast the sword away. When Bedivere confessed that he had not fulfilled the command, Arthur rebuked him and insisted that Excalibur must be returned.

Finally, Bedivere carried Excalibur to the edge of the lake. With great sorrow, he hurled the sword into the water. As the sword touched the surface, a hand clad in white silk emerged from the depths, caught the sword by the hilt, and then disappeared beneath the waves, taking Excalibur back to its mystical origin. Bedivere returned to Arthur, who was now near death. Arthur, knowing that his end was imminent, instructed Bedivere to

take him to a nearby shore where a boat awaited. This boat was manned by three mysterious queens, dressed in black, who were said to be sorceresses. These queens were the sisters of Avalon, a mystical isle where the ancient dead were taken for healing and rest.

With Bedivere's help, Arthur was placed in the boat, and the queens set sail for Avalon. As the boat drifted away, Arthur spoke his final words to Bedivere, expressing his hope that he would be healed in Avalon and might return one day to rule again. The boat vanished into the mist, leaving Bedivere alone on the shore, mourning the loss of his king.

After Arthur's departure, Bedivere wandered the land in despair, unsure of what the future held. The knights of the Round Table were gone, Camelot lay in ruins, and the kingdom was left without its leader. Arthur's death marked the end of an era—the fall of Camelot and the passing of the golden age of chivalry.

Yet, the legend of King Arthur did not end with his death. It was said that Arthur was not truly dead but merely sleeping in Avalon, waiting for the day when Britain would need him once more. This hope kept the spirit of Arthur alive in the hearts of his people, and the promise of his return became a beacon in the dark times that followed.

Main image: *The Passing of Arthur* by Stella Langdale, circa 1920s; **Above:** *The Passing of Arthur* by Richard Hope, 1925

INDEX

PICTURE CREDITS AND ACKNOWLEDGEMENTS

The majority of the pictures used here are in the public domain, but in all cases are courtesy of the following institutions, organisations, and individuals: Trinity College Dublin; The National Library of Ireland, Dublin; The National Museum of Ireland, Dublin; The National Museum of Denmark, Copenhagen; The British Museum; The Royal Cornwall Museum; The Brú na Bóinne complex, County Meath, Ireland; The British Library; National Galleries of Scotland; The State Archaeological Collection, Munich Narodni muzeum, Prague, Czech Republic; The Museum of the Middle Ages, Paris, France; Musée St. Remi, Reims, France; The Royal Irish Academy Library, Dublin; Glenveagh National Park, Donegal; Axa Briga Park, Settimo Rottaro, Italy; The Metropolitan Museum of Art, New York City; Museum of the Middle Ages, Paris, France; Walters Art Museum, Mount Vernon, Baltimore; Art Renewal Center of New Jersey (ARC); Mary Evans Picture Library; Alamy; Picryl, the public domain search & similarity engine; Wikipedia; Wiki Commons; Shutterstock; Adobe Stock; Fine Art Images; Old World Gods; Roman-Britain.co.uk; Notre Dame de Bulat church, Bulat Pestivien, Cotes d'Armor, Brittany; Musée des Beaux Arts, Quimper, Brittany, France; Clonfert Cathedral, County Galway, Ireland; Gallerie di Piazza Scala, Milano; Landesmuseum Württemberg, Stuttgart; Cambodunum Archaeological Park in Kempten, Schwaben, Southern Germany; Alignments de Kerlescan, at Carnac, Brittany; *Luccio Darezzo* on DeviantArt; Avid Archer; St. Gwyddelan's Church, Dolwyddelan, Gwynedd; George Philip & Son Ltd for The London Geographical Institute; North Wind Picture Archives on Alamy; *any_s_kill* at DeviantArt; *IonicAI* at DeviantArt; *Your Irish*; Kingdom Poets, by D.S. Martin: *Sweeney Astray*; *Leabhar Breac*; Celtic Native; Irish Heritage News; Meet the Myths; Christine Dorman, moonfishwriting.com; *Brehon Academy*; Paganista; *Irish History*; *Ireland's Lore and Tales* on Wordpress; Ann Massey McElroy, *Dark Emerald Tales & Travels*; Siegfried Rabanser, via Wikimedia Commons; Reddit/Eldon Bling courtesy of *Kevin's Ireland*; Jennifer Derrig/*The Irish Jewelry Company*; Eoin McConnell on Alamy; *Irishhistory*; Anikó Salamon; *Luna Moonfall* at Nightcafe Studio; "The Plan of Tara," based on a survey of the site and historical records, drawn by William Wakeman and published in Wakeman's Handbook of Irish Antiquities, 1903; Danebury Hillfort, Hampshire, England; *Llyn Tegid* (Bala Lake), Gwynedd; The Seed Company; and Sarah Young

With thanks to the painters, sculptors, and artists whose pictures we have used: Stephen Reid; Stella Langdale; Beatrice Elvery; Arthur Rackham; John Duncan; Christopher Williams; Alan Lee; Howard Pyle; Gustave Doré; William Dyce; Edward Burne-Jones; William Blake; Richard Hope; William Bell Scott; John Garrick; James Archer; William Hatherell; Emil Doepler; John Bauer; Arthur Hacker; WJ Enright; Eric Pape; George Frederic Watts RA; Albert Herter; Newell Convers Wyeth; Arthur Hughes; Edmund Dulac; Louis Rhead; Eleanor Fortesque-Brickdale; Emil Johann Lauffer; W. Benda; Richard Westall RA; Frederick Sandys; Charles Ernest Butler RA; Frank William Warwick Topham; André Castaigne; François-Louis Dejuinne; Évariste Vital Luminai; Alfred Quinton; John Reinhard Weguelin; R. Doyle; Herbert James Draper; John William Waterhouse; Edmund Leighton; Rogelio de Egusquiza; Alfred Fredericks; Thomas Heath Robinson; Peter Diamond; Henry Charles Fehr; David Jones; Hugh Frazer; Henry Justice Ford; François Gérard; J. C. Leyendecker; E. Wallcousins; Helen Stratton; George Denham; John D. Batten; H. R. Millar; Henry Fuseli; Thomas Crofton Croker; (A drawing in the style of Richard Dadd) by J. Arnold, and engraved on wood by Henry Lynton; Sophie Anderson; Bartolomeo Giuliano; Joseph Paton; John Darren Sutton; Lionel Royer; Aimé Millet; Harry Payne; J. Rogers; and finally, Maud Gonne, for *The Coming of Lugh*, retold by Ella Young and published in 1909 by Maunsel & Co., Dublin